T0194954

NONE LIKE HER

Awaken the Beauty within You

Sandra L. Coates

WESTBOW
PRESS®
A DIVISION OF THOMAS NELSON
& ZONDERVAN

WestBow Press books may be ordered through booksellers or by contacting:

WestBow Press
A Division of Thomas Nelson & Zondervan
1663 Liberty Drive
Bloomington, IN 47403
www.westbowpress.com
844-714-3454

ISBN: 978-1-6642-3962-3 (sc)
ISBN: 978-1-6642-3963-0 (hc)
ISBN: 978-1-6642-3961-6 (e)

Library of Congress Control Number: 2021913739

Print information available on the last page.

WestBow Press rev. date: 8/18/2021

CONTENTS

This book is dedicated to the God who has always known of my beauty and graciously chose to tell me one holy whisper at a time. I am in awe of Your splendor within me that compels me to rise up, stand tall and tell the world.

Until she knows there is none like her …

WHAT READERS ARE SAYING :

Once I started, I couldn't stop! Sandra was so on point and I felt like I was reading a book about my life. Every scenario, every story resonated with me and I could see myself in each part. Sandra's honesty, truth and biblical examples brought realness and understanding of how I could apply it to my own life. If you are trying to figure out your purpose or your part in this world, this book will bring to life what God has in you.

(Morgan Hart- Brand Designer/Entrepreneur, Creative Designer for Tamra Andress, Co-Pastor)

None like her is a must read for every woman and girl! Sandra is such an inspiration as she vulnerably shares her story of finding the true beauty that God placed within her. My hope and prayer as you read this book is that you too will be inspired and know you are worthy, loved and called just the way you are.

(Tiffany Rogers- Mrs. Virginia 2020; Founder of Hope 4 Healing)

None Like Her" is something every woman can relate to. It nails the fact that God made you purposefully unique. This book is a great tool to reinforce our identity in Christ and hush the lies of the enemy. Teens, moms, wives, sisters and daughters - know that you are carefully and wonderfully made and there is NONE LIKE YOU

(Angela L. W. McDowell, MA, MMFT Co-founder of Marriage MAPP)

Sandra's book hits the mark regarding the juxtaposition of our current culture's view of women's beauty, worth and success versus the One who created us, sees us and longs to be in close relationship with us. She has accomplished this through her beautiful vulnerability, sharing her hard fought battles against culture's shallow offerings, and by allowing God to replace each lie regarding women's worth with His view of her true worth.

(-Shannon Elrod, RN, FNP, DNP)

This book has no barriers of connectivity: no matter age, ethnicity, or economic differences. Sandra's stories, though different from mine, hit a familiar pit in my stomach. Isolation and perfectionism plague many of His precious gems and yet in submission and prayer He restores our shine. Thank you for rising up to serve His daughters from the very place Satan has tried to take.

(Tamra Andress -Christian Business Coach, Globally Ranked Podcast Host: Fit in Faith Podcast, Ordained Minister, Author & Speaker)

The book has the ability to change lives! It hits all the major insecurities every girl faces and fights it with biblical truth. It shows us how to put on and use the armor of God to fight off the enemy and come out victorious. The book brings to light the enemy's deceiving tactics and gives not only practical ways to conquer but also gives us scripture to back it up! Sandra puts Jesus at the center and gives Him all the glory.

(Gracie Goodwin- Liberty University college student/ Student Leader)

None Like Her is a touching story with an urgent message. It's personal, freeing and undeniably true. Even more, None Like Her is transformative. Most of us ladies are secretly chained to feelings of unworthiness– of not measuring up. Sandra redefines beauty and reminds us of the unique perfection God lavished upon each of us. Every girl, woman and mom needs to know God made... None Like Her.

(Carey Lewis -Founder of Actors, Models & Talent for Christ (AMTC); SHINE by Carey Lewis)

"A very timely read for women in this day and age! This book is timeless but also purposeful for what women are truly up against today when it comes to finding their purpose, value, and identity. This book is a tool for women to learn how to put aside a worldly perspective and teach them to hold the truth of God who will then realign, nourish, heal, and strengthen broken areas and breathe new life into them."

(Kristi Anderson- Professional Angler ; Owner
and Founder of 1Fish2Fish LLC)

Sandra's ability to be vulnerable, authentic and transparent is inspiring! Her story will resonate with so many others who can relate to the painful journey of a child and young adult, especially dealing with issues around body image and confidence. The hope she infuses as she discovers God's plan for her is a powerful hope others can embrace for themselves.

(L. Diane Wagenhals- M.Ed- Lakeside Global Institute Program
Director -specializing in trauma research and curriculum)

"I've battled insecurities and doubted my worth since I was a young girl. Reading this powerful book changed my perspective on where true beauty resides. Sandra's writing is jam-packed with valuable tools on how to transform the way you view yourself and embrace your God-given beauty to change the world."

(-Arjola Mullaj- Regent University college student/ Young Life leader)

Sandra shares her relatable journey with honesty and the hope of encouraging others who have struggled with body image, eating disorders and anxiety. It is a beautiful, personal story of hope, learning to like and love yourself and who God has created you to be, in His image!

(Becky VanValin LCSW; Therapist and Owner at Eden Counseling)

"None Like Her has earth-shattering truths that defeat the constant mental attacks single women, like me, have experienced and wake up the beautiful warrior. In such a relatable way, Sandra humbly shares her experiences reminding us that it is our Heavenly Father who has the last say so about our inward and outward beauty; not anyone or anything else. This book challenges us to avoid making perfection the goal. The real goal for all of us is to embrace our God-assigned worth and make a decision every day to walk confidently in it."

(-Vernicia T. Eure, MA,CT; Relationship Coach; Author, Stepping Into Purity)

"As a girl dad who recognizes the need for women to know their true worth in all stages of life, 'None Like Her' speaks to the heart of what that's supposed to look like. This is a real, transparent look at Sandra's self-acceptance journey, as well as her acceptance of who God made her to be."

(-Saulo Ortiz, LCSW ; Founder of Life Change Institute)

"I have known Sandra for almost 25 years and watched first hand as she helped awaken young women to see their purpose and worth. Simple and powerful, this book has the potential to transform as it shares the message of identity found in God's design."

(Pete Hardesty, Young Life College Divisional Coordinator; co-author of Amazon #1 bestsellers Adulting 101 Book 1 and Book 2)

PREFACE

What if you never had to chase beauty again?

This book is for women who want to know the greatness that exists inside of them, to break free of who they thought they had to be, and stand securely in the identity they've always had—treasured and fiercely loved without ever having to do anything. I might not know your name, your culture, or your story, but I do know this: You hold value and purpose that no other woman has. You aren't here by accident. You were planned for and made in the image of the same Creator who painted the skies and called the waves to crash, the birds to sing, and the mountains to display their majesty.

Maybe, like me, you need to know that you really have a royal inheritance embedded inside your soul. It's been there since you were knit together in your mother's womb, and it holds power that is good, dangerously good.

Where you have come from is only part of your story, with every possibility to be transformed into something brand new by a God, who never stops working on your behalf. Despite the opposition against you, you must know the truth: You are never too far gone, too old, too young, or too unprepared for God to do something amazing in your life. You have a voice. You have a platform. You don't need more influence; you are already known as part of the masterpiece. All of it was given to you to live out your exact story and use it to show others the grandeur of more, more than this world has to offer. This kind of beauty within us shouts of a master designer who beckons you to believe and embrace what He says about you.

"Before you were born, I set you apart" (Jeremiah 1:5 NIV).

Society's measuring stick of beauty has become the standard; this resulted in an epidemic, a great battle attacking females of all ages, and it is killing us. The pressure to be perfect, live perfect, earn your beauty, be outwardly flawless and followed by the world, shouts at us, to no avail. We keep chasing and comparing, staring at idols with what appears to be helping us achieve a set of goals but somehow never freeing us from the very thing we want. In our culture today, this crisis of our identity as females seems to swing the pendulum to either side. One is filled with valuing the supremacy of self, worship of position or power, while the other is laden with unworthiness and shame, self-loathing, and feelings of inadequacy. Regardless of where you fall, it was never supposed to be this way.

If we, as the King's daughters, can know who we are and live united and free, our strength will be unstoppable. When we realize this truth, then we become a beautiful force to be reckoned with. Bethany Hamilton, author of *Soul Surfer* and *Unstoppable* and a professional surfer who became famous after losing an arm in a shark attack, has this to say about life: "I don't need easy, I just need possible." (bethanyhamilton.com)

In American culture today, there's quite a big focus on women's empowerment, the unprecedented strength of females with abilities comparable to the strongest of superheroes. We do hold more power and purpose than we realize or are given credit for. The question then becomes, what are we called to do with it? While the world beckons us to chase an illusion to be perfect, fearless, more accomplished, or more

What if the greatest part about us was what we let go of, rather than what we held on to?

influential, there lies a balance with our humanness and who we were meant to be. What if the greatest part about us was what we let go of, rather than what we held on to? What if we held a beauty unlike any other woman on earth and a destiny written for the kingdom to come? What if we had new weapons to fight with? Better yet, what if the battles we face are not ours to fight?

God has given me a burning desire to see every woman and girl break free from society's beauty standards of who she thought she was supposed to be and step into the grandeur of the beauty she already possesses. It is my prayer to encourage and empower women in this epic battle of worth, as beauty is redefined to take her deeper inside the war for her destination, to see herself as God sees her: breathtaking, confident, and uniquely beautiful, despite the battle scars she bears.

I long for this generation around the globe to know their beauty, their value, and their power to change the world. I'm so excited to have you on this journey because you, my friend, are a beautiful warrior with sacred battle scars and a story to prove it. There is simply no one like you.

INTRODUCTION

▍DIGGING UP ME

I always wanted to be comfortable in my own skin, but any glimpse of it was so fleeting. An encouraging word, a surprise compliment, or feeling the success of an accomplishment proved to be a temporary joy that quickly vanished. If I saw an unflattering picture of myself (apart from cute and chubby baby pictures), I would be mortified and vow to never eat again. The glimmers of good always seemed to be drowned out by the ongoing sea of criticisms, negative thought patterns, and a constant need to prove myself. I so wanted to fit in. I wouldn't say it out loud, but I made it my goal to be perfect and feel confident and content in who I was. Somehow, I believed that if I could chase after perfection in the things I could control, then the things I couldn't change wouldn't be a constant reminder of failure. It was subtle and sneaky and never ending. A deep thread of failure was weaving its way into areas of my life that I longed to be different.

In this journey, I had to find me, the real me, who had been crafted from the beginning with purpose and a story to live out loud. Many challenges had come up against me, trying to sabotage the story and suppress all that was within me. The solution was not about the right friends or job or relationship, but about learning who the real me was: a delighted woman of God with no apologies and no agenda. I needed to see the war that was after my God-given place as His chosen warrior to stand strong. Known for being super tall, left-handed, with giant feet and a people-pleasing spirit, I realized that it was my instant response to run and hide when pain hit. Some knew me as intimidating and others as kind and friendly. Instead of fully embracing one of those personas, I learned to be a chameleon.

All along, I thought I was the only one who was restless and longing for more out of life, relationships, careers and the passions within me. I thought I was the only one who questioned why I didn't like who I was or why I wasn't fulfilled in this land of plenty. The to-do lists, titles after our name, engagement rings, and dream houses can't silence the nagging ache for something that will satisfy forever. I've always wanted to lead a fun life of adventure and purpose that thrills and satisfies my inner free spirit but still keeps me responsible and grounded. Somehow, it all gets complicated, and I wrestle with who I was really meant to be. We have to know we are loved completely before we can know ourselves and learn our place in this life.

Discovering who I really was would change everything, and I found a stronger, more satisfied woman, one who craved more of God, who offered me the radiance I longed for. It was in the struggle, in the drought and darkest hours that I began to see new and lasting hope really was alive, and it was for me. Beyond all of my failed attempts and painful obstacles, there was one stronger who saw through my struggle. He was the God of miracles, who did the impossible in my life story. And just as He did for me, He wants to take you from a place of "I can't" to the victory of "I can," from the drought to the delighted place where new life can grow and flourish at the appointed time.

> **Beyond all of my failed attempts and painful obstacles, there was one stronger who saw through my struggle.**

Why would I even attempt to write a book? To me, there is nothing scarier or more intimidating. It seems like it's the thing to do; everyone wants to write a book and tell their stories nowadays. Why would mine be any different? But what compels me to sit down and write these words is that others out there may feel the same way I do: hungry for something more, searching for refuge from the war inside that threatens her very soul. Maybe they too have experienced a battle to find true confidence, peace, security, and purpose. Like me, they may wear bold words on their T-shirt, listen to empowering speakers, or even coach others on these same topics, but inside, there may still be that aching question: Do I have what it takes? Am I really beautiful? Could God's power and love really penetrate my guarded heart, which has been hurt time and time again? Will I ever not feel overlooked or unfulfilled? How do I stop trying to be perfect? Why is being a woman so complicated?

Some of us have felt the stigma of our outward appearance. We lacked something, or something was different about us that caused stares and rumors or prejudice against us. We may not have done anything to our looks or to bring on the mocking of others, but the emotionally weighted impact has shaped our understanding of ourselves and others. Others may have always been known for our outward beauty, praised for our looks or our abilities, and expected to constantly perform or meet expectations. We may feel pressure towards perfection or feel the internal need to compete with other girls or to draw attention by standing out somehow. We may feel so far gone that all we want to do is hide. Regardless of where we are, the mirror has been groomed as a dictator for far too long.

Wherever you've been, it's time to know the epic story set out just for you.

PART 1

My Story, Her Story

EXPOSING ROOTS

As the bus pulled away from the school, the driver's message rang over the speaker loud and clear: "Whatever you do, stay seated in your assigned seat." It echoed throughout the bus. She finished her script, pausing in between reminders for the giggling fifth graders in the back to stop their talking and listen to her words. My seat was in the front section, with the other first graders. As the ride continued, we weaved in and out of neighborhoods, dropping kids off, and the seats began clearing out.

All of a sudden, the bus came to a screeching halt, and the driver grabbed the intercom mic with an angry scowl. "You better *sit* down," she yelled, looking in my direction.

It was almost impossible to see her eyes behind her tinted sunglasses. I looked around the bus; I was one of the only kids left in the front, so I straightened up to pay more attention. I was a rule follower and had been compliant the whole ride, so surely she wasn't talking to me.

She spoke once again: "You in the third row. I can see your head over the seat. You better sit down, or I will not be moving this bus."

My face suddenly flushed with fear and confusion as I realized she *was* talking to me. But I was sitting in my seat. I was so tall, especially for my age, that it appeared I was standing up instead of sitting, as she had warned. I ducked my head, and the tears began to flow. They continued for the rest of the ride home, while I hid behind the big black seat so she wouldn't see my head.

After bawling my eyes out to my mom that afternoon, it was clear I had a defender. Her momma bear instinct marched down to the bus stop the next morning only to exchange some fiery words to the bus driver about my height and the huge mistake that had happened that previous afternoon. Little did I know the battle that would begin that early. I would need defending.

Ever since I was a little girl, I wanted to be beautiful. Let me clarify: I wanted to *feel* beautiful and feel free to be myself with those around me. Ultimately, I wanted to be beautiful in their eyes. In my mind, if the world thought I was beautiful, then it would really be true (not just my mom saying it because she sees through those "mom" glasses). I longed for a beauty that was visible to everyone. Little did I know that there would be an all-out war for the very essence of who I was; eventually, I discovered the true meaning of the beauty I really did possess. I always tried to cover up my large size; I always appeared to look older than I was but never measured up to the standard set. For so long, I never wanted to be in pictures because I didn't think I looked beautiful; I certainly didn't look like the popular girls in school or on the magazine rack.

I wanted to bow down to what others praised as pretty and successful and confident, but the reminders of failing those standards kept coming. The theme was, you're too big for your size, you eat too much, and you're fat; therefore, your looks don't cut it, and you're not strong enough to stand up for yourself when someone criticizes you. The bottom line: You're marked with flaws and scars that remind you of your failed attempts to fly, and you can't change it. It felt like a permanent prison sentence.

Just before middle school, I asked for Richard Simmons's health and fitness program, complete with the recipe book; this was going to be my ticket to success. In my mind, I would achieve my skinny and happy goals in no time. After the box came, I marveled at all the delicious recipes and was very eager to start. My family announced we were taking a dream vacation to Hawaii that summer, and I had a glorious plan that was going to make all of my problems disappear. By this time, I was two hundred pounds and about five feet, nine inches tall. The problem was, my plan didn't work. I quit after the first day because I didn't know how to fight something that held so much power over me and had been filling my needs, at least temporarily, for all this time. It was going to stay a dream I had wished would come true, but my body would continue to show evidence of a war happening inside for quite some time.

THE BIG GIRL

We lined up for our annual sports physicals at school; there I was, sandwiched in between all the girls half my size. I tried not to care, but all I could see was all the things I wasn't; the body I didn't have that screamed at me. I felt disqualified before anything even began.

The protocol began: "OK, girls, take your shoes off and make sure you stand up straight so we can get accurate heights and weights. Next in line …"

On those days, I desperately wished I had a doctor's appointment or was home sick, unable to attend the torturous event. As I approached the dreaded scale, I anticipated a crash when I stepped onto the wiggly black platform. I could feel the silence along with all the eyes on me. The nurse, who was always notoriously smaller than I was, would stare at the numbers before her and make adjustments. She gave me a quick glance up and down as she tried to maneuver around my large frame. She kept moving the top weight farther and farther down the notches, to try and balance out the completely tipped scale. As she slowly found the final number, the embarrassment filled me. Inside, I wanted to protest because this couldn't be true; I was heavier than last time, but I had no defense for my case. My scale at home was at least five pounds lighter; this one must've been broken.

I was prepared for the letdown, contrary to all the other normal-sized girls before and after me, who just seemed to glide through this process with ease. But something always died inside of me. I wanted to grab that paper, scratch my name out, and tear the whole thing to shreds. I was mortified. Exposed. Defeated. I couldn't escape the competition of comparison, and I was too weak in confidence to see anything but failure. I felt the silent judgment all around me, and the labels were embedded deeper in me. Why was this such a struggle for me? What was I doing wrong? Why had I been cursed by being so big? I felt so stuck, and I hated my body.

I didn't fit the mold. I inherited my height from my grandfather, who was six feet, five inches and had gigantic feet. My size raised questions and wrinkled noses. I wanted to be small, skinny, and confident in my own skin, free to laugh at life. I wanted to know what it was like to go into a store and buy clothes in the size I was supposed to be or find the shoes that all my friends had. Comparison became something that was bred in me since I can remember. It went beyond my large frame. It was an ongoing battle, and every day, I wished it would go away. The idea of being popular at school or just not getting asked a million questions about my size was out of the question. I remember being at home, thumbing through my favorite magazines and tearing out pictures of girls I wanted to be like. Inside I wanted to have their life and not mine because they were skinny, they were popular, and they looked strong, confident, and free. To me, they didn't have a care in the world. Although I was only a young girl, the deep roots of comparison and envy had begun to form. Oh, to be like her would be so much better.

I always wanted to be esteemed by others. My lifelong ambition centered around reaching higher and higher goals. Pretty quickly, I realized life was going to be a constant fight of who I dreamed to be versus the reality show around me that brought its share of pain, competition, and a reputation that was often chosen for me. I got good at hiding and telling white lies to sound better, feel safer, and hopefully become more likeable (well, at least temporarily, until the competition was back).

Something in me wanted to fight back, but society's beauty standards always seemed unattainable in this battle. Without even trying, my inside voice would remind me, *She's the pretty one, not you. She's smart, not you. She's the real athlete, not you. She chooses who she dates, not you. Her family is intact, and they enjoy time together, unlike yours. You are at church all the time and do all these activities, but it's not enough to fill you.* It's only a matter of time until you realize your identity is not just about you. It is spoken and shaped by influences around you that you can't control.

I was reminded of the above as a young girl, when I couldn't fit in the ballet leotard or the shiny black shoes with the pretty black ribbon. It continued as a teenager when my thighs constantly rubbed together and I got called names for being big, or when my friends at the sleepover were comparing belly buttons on their beautiful washboard abs, while I was outfitted with cellulite and stretch marks. I continually felt that my core identity was less valuable than my peers, so I had to find another way to be noticed, to possess something attractive about myself.

I finally found something I could do and held onto it for dear life. I became immersed in sports and loved pleasing people. Subsequently, I began craving every ounce of acceptance and accolades I could get. All the kids in my neighborhood joined the local swim team and spent the summer at the swim club. Every morning, we would ride our bikes to swim practice and then stay the day as one of the pool rats. With the smell of chlorine and sunscreen wafting in the air, we took breaks from the pool to hang out by the snack bar, play cards, and make bracelets.

I remember one particular instance of lies that covered my ugly truth. It happened when a boy noticed my stretch marks and asked, "What are those red lines on your back?"

The stress and panic of embarrassment immediately came over me. Maybe he wasn't talking to me, but then I realized I was found out. Exposed.

I responded, "Oh those? My cat scratched me."

Now a group of poolmates and their friends stepped in for a closer look. I felt the panic growing and wanted to crawl in a hole.

"Those aren't cat scratches," another boy announced as he studied my back. "What are they?"

Feeling the weight of my own shame and secrecy, I tried to deflect the conversation and blurted out, "I don't know; they're strange marks, OK?"

People saw I was visibly upset, so the barrage of questions thankfully ceased, and everyone departed. But moments like these became my norm. Stretch marks were a constant reminder that I needed to hide myself to try to fit in. I didn't see any other girls with big red ugly marks, and I certainly didn't see anyone who looked like me. Inside, I felt like I had a disease, and it began to shape me, cause me to second-guess myself and wonder when the next round of interrogation or rejection would come.

It wasn't just my peers; it was other parents, teachers, coaches, and friends who talked more about my size than any other trait. I was a giant among all the other girls, and I had to fight through the stares and comments of being seen. It felt risky, so I had to give it my all, every time I got the chance.

I would stand on the starting block of a swim race, with a girl half my size on either side of me, but somehow block them out because I had my eye on the finish line. With a belly-flop start and a large body, my eight-and-under self managed to do something wonderful. I was actually good at swimming, in spite of my size. In fact, my size and the small voice of competition within me started to bring forth the confidence I never knew I had. Could my size actually be a good thing for once in my life, instead of a spectacle to gawk at or joke about?

Somehow, the negative of being seen in a bathing suit was overcome by the feeling of being good at something. I received the title of "Whopper Queen" because I belly flopped instead of diving off the starting block. To my surprise, I won a lot of races and displayed the colorful ribbons and trophies all over my room. I always dreaded the swim team picture, where everything was highlighted on my body, but I smiled and gave it my best. I soon realized that I could successfully live a double life. There was the life I lived in public through sports, and there was the life I lived full of shame on the inside.

In his book *Emotionally Healthy Spirituality,* author and pastor Paul Scazzero writes about this tendency we all have to hide when our emotional selves are not being cared for. He says, "Pretending was safer than honesty and vulnerability." While living my double life, I didn't realize that there was a God who knew every thought and every wish and every hurt that I'd ever gone through. I never dreamed He would one day sew those tattered pieces back together and make them beautiful. Deep within, the warrior was already in training.

THE BEGINNING MARKS

I grew up in a Christian home; we went to church every Sunday and during the week. We were known as a strong, faith-filled family, and I had no reason to believe otherwise. My sister was two years older than me, and I strived to be like her in every way possible. She was smart, she was pretty, and she didn't struggle with her weight. Although she had shortcomings and fought her own battles, in my eyes, she was the coolest. She was the best at basically everything. She was a stellar student with a drive and a confidence that I wanted but never seemed to possess. She let criticism roll off her back and silenced her opposition in one strike. Her handwriting was always so much better than mine; I was left-handed and not as neat. I was also a free spirit and not detail oriented.

To top it all off, I was disastrously fragile and sensitive. Not a good combination for anyone. What made things more complicated was the fact that my parents divorced when I was eleven and about to enter middle school. My sister and I were completely blindsided by the news because, in our eyes, we were a pretty normal family. Just weeks before the painful announcement, we had gone on a dream vacation and had baked my parents a surprise cake for their anniversary. Little did we know that their split was imminent. My dad had decided to divorce my mom, but tried to convince us that nothing would change with us, except his physical address. He attempted to remain active in our lives, but no matter what he did, it just wasn't the same. I had always been very close to Dad and had received love, assurance, and confidence from him. I tried my best to appear that everything was going to be OK, just as he had said, but the problem with that was, everything *wasn't* OK. At the sheer pain of being left, fear and loneliness shouted louder and louder inside.

Love became unpredictable for me. It was too dangerous to fight for because of the sting that came with it. As I watched my mom grieve her broken marriage and hurting daughters, I felt even worse. I tried so hard to be brave, but inside I, too, was broken. How could this be our new normal? It was unfinished; a weight of bills and loss of security now awaited me. While growing up, I learned great fundamentals about God's love and the importance of a church community. But that all seemed powerless after the divorce. I begged God to put our family back together and be normal again. Only He knew the depth of my pain while I hid behind smiles and tried to act like all was well.

I kept a collage of old pictures of my mom and dad when they were young; they seemed happy and in love. It all seemed real for a time, or so I thought. What I didn't realize was the fact that God was using my pain as a platform for redemption and beauty. I would need God more than ever now, but it would take a while to get there. I began to look everywhere else for the love and security I needed.

Through counseling, mentors, and life experiences, I began to understand our family unit and realized my parents had their own personal struggles. So often, we just don't know the impact of our own past hurts. My dad, an only child from a broken home with his own set of scars, would never know the influence he held in our family and the wreckage he caused. My mom, who dealt with her own panic disorder, had trauma and shame that tainted her life from an early age. Years later, God would boldly use her greatest pains as a platform to help others deal with trauma in their past experiences.

Over the course of my childhood, I often wanted to be someone different, someone new. I never wanted to be the girl everyone looked at and felt sorry for. I didn't want to have to always think of my size and worry about how I compared to everyone else. I didn't want it to define me. When I was a young girl, the movie *Big* with Tom Hanks came out. I remember something glorious sparked in me as I watched that movie. I wished and dreamed of how wonderful it would be to put my token into the genie's machine and have my wish granted to be small. I wanted to feel free in a normal-sized body, without question of how old I was, or why was I as tall as our schoolteachers. I was the outlier, and it was a lonely, anxiety-producing spot I was stuck in that tainted almost everything. Self-confidence was something I never experienced, apart from what I could achieve. No one told me to hide, but it felt better when I did.

I was not what I was expected to be.

As life continued, so did my size. I was labeled "obese" by the growth charts and stood out to anyone and everyone. I was miserable. I was not what I was expected to be. My parents both tried hard to shield me from it all. My mom was always trying to praise me and encourage me, and my dad would tell me I looked pretty and was a good athlete. But inside, I was fragile; I desperately wanted people to notice good things about me. Since I couldn't do anything about the reality of my size, I put enormous amounts of energy into what others said about me, especially teachers, coaches, and peers I looked up to in school. I gave them permission to speak into the deepest parts of me. Sometimes, it lifted me up, while other times, it cut even deeper. I couldn't stop the longing for more affirmation. I wanted encouragement and validation; I'd hang onto their every word. Although I was fully immersed in the culture of sports at school and being the best I could be, it just wasn't enough. I still remember the comment my high school coach made in front of a whole group of my peers one day before the bell rang to leave class: "Hey, Sandra, what are you going to do to keep that weight down now that field hockey season is over?"

I was not ready for his prickly comment in the midst of small talk by the classroom door among friends. Feeling the angst of embarrassment, I just couldn't pretend that it didn't bother me. *Who does he think he is?*

With everyone still standing there, I shot him a look of disgust and fired back, "For your information, I've already started my swim season, and we're in the pool practicing every day."

He offered a smirk and responded, "Oh, well, that's good."

I was voted "Most Athletic Girl" in my graduating class, which was quite an honor after all the seasons and injuries I endured, but unfortunately, it only lasted a short time. None of the trophies and recognition could fix me. I was still angry, broken, fragile, and continually reminded of the battle to keep proving myself. As I moved into adulthood, I brought those wounds with me, and they affected other areas of my life, even though I no longer competed as an athlete. The roots of rejection and insecurity were embedded deeper than I could reach; I couldn't do anything about them. They weren't just affecting my circumstances, but instead were attacking me. It didn't matter that I had moved into new seasons or completed impressive goals; something was tinting my lenses to see. Phrases such as "You don't have what it takes," and "You're not enough," and "I hate my size," were etched into my brain as a permanent filter that I experienced everything through.

SINKING

As a new college student, I was determined not to gain the "freshman fifteen." I wanted so much to have a new start. But unfortunately, my habits hadn't changed, and I was still on the run from God. It was just me, trying to do life as best as I knew how. I could not see the relevance of involving God in my life because I had so many things I wanted to do, and I believed His ways would hold me back. I played sports, so carb-loading parties and weight training regimes were needed in order to keep up muscle, energy, and stamina to perform at the highest level possible. I went to a prestigious university in Philadelphia, and I received a scholarship to swim for a Division 1 school. I felt I had finally reached a dream, and everything was going to finally fall into place. It felt good to be chosen.

Ironically, it was there that my swimming career came to a halt, and things started to fall apart. I quickly realized I wasn't a front-runner or even a key contributor to the team. I was just another swimmer who was barely recognized and fought a lot of uphill battles to stay mentally focused, just in case I was needed for a relay. I was used to athletic success in high school, the legacies, trophies, coaches, and teammates who made it great. I thought surely those accolades would serve as a secure platform to stand on.

I tried to find myself again and realized I needed to make a change. Sports weren't filling me, and neither was my longtime boyfriend nor new college experiences. But what else was there? One day, during my freshman year, while sitting in my dorm room, I felt miserable. Nothing was enough anymore, and I had become desperate. That was when I heard a still small voice whisper inside, *I have more for you than this*. I didn't know who or what that was, but I could not stop thinking about it. I did want more, but how? For so long, my identity, drive, and validation came from a playing field with a scoreboard, a pool, and a trophy case. I was programmed to strive hard and prove (to myself and to others) that I was going to succeed at whatever I started. Now what did I have to show for myself? I was going to lose all that I thought was my success; I'd probably never be invited to another college party again.

As these nagging thoughts continued to surface, I decided to close the chapter and take a leap. Some would call it my faith, but I found out later it was a gracious heavenly Father who was wooing me away from myself and toward something real and lasting that would soon set me free. For the first time, I wasn't going to be known for my performance or my name.

I left my home state of Pennsylvania and transferred to a small college in Virginia. Starting off my sophomore year at a new school, in a new state, with no sport to train for or title after my name, I was determined to *be* something. I chose "skinny." So I tried a new eating plan starting off that year, and it worked. It was the "starve yourself until you're not hungry for food anymore" diet. It was basically anorexia, but I didn't see it that way and was glad to feel something exciting again. I dropped roughly twenty-five pounds from the time school started in August until fall break. It felt amazing on the outside, as I wore sizes I never dreamed possible. Unfortunately, on the inside, I was unhealthy and still suffering from the same loneliness, insecurity, and deep-seated fears of being alone or rejected. I was searching.

I struggled with the same issue by using food to control something I couldn't find on my own. Only this time, I used it as a weapon to gain control of my appearance, and I liked it. It was mind over matter, and eventually, I stopped being hungry. I remember feeling the euphoria when I was called "skinny" for the first time and the identity I believed came with it. I had never felt desired for my physical frame or noted for being thin. Maybe I had finally arrived, or so I thought.

It caught up with me after a while, since the angst of food around me was still an ongoing war of self-sabotage. If I was left alone, it would be nothing for me to secretly gorge a large intake of food or figure out a way to hide. I'd immediately feel the shame and not be able to make myself throw up. I hated vomiting more than anything, so I chose to over-exercise at all hours of the night in order to try and burn off the excess calories I had consumed. But I was never happy about it. I was always "the project who could do better." It became my obsession.

As I recall, I was still quite vulnerable to binges. I'd often push myself not to eat. One time, I found a half-eaten piece of pizza sitting in a box in the trash can of the girls' bathroom in my dorm hall. I was hungry and had barely eaten anything. I grabbed that piece of a stranger's pizza from the garbage and hid in the bathroom stall to scarf it down. After I ate it, the shame immediately came over me, and I wanted to throw it all up. How could I stop the war with food and feel free instead? I wanted to be in control, desirable, and disciplined, like so many others around me appeared to be. I was the epitome of trapped and desperate.

This particular low point in my life reminds me of the biblical parable of the prodigal son (I like to rephrase it as the prodigal daughter) in Luke 15. He also wanted to control his life and found himself alone and desperate. He didn't know where his source of safety and unconditional love came from, until all he had was gone. As he found himself with nothing left, "longing to fill his stomach with the pods the pigs were eating" (Luke 15:15 NIV), he began to see more clearly. He didn't know his father, who he had left with his inheritance, had been longing to rescue him the whole time.

Unbeknownst to me, I had started using food to numb painful and empty places as far back as I can remember. I longed to feel love and pleasure. I could trace it back to one of those dreaded swim team pictures. As I studied the picture, I was immediately filled with the pain from that time of my life and realized that was the same year that my dad left our family. Even though my mom tried to press forward in survival, the lasting effects tainted everything. My mom, my sister, and I were left to try and do life as we did before, but we were all grieving in our own way. I myself was desperate to feel love and wholeness again, and food fit the bill at the time. I stared at the overweight, short-haired, eleven-year-old me, and my heart broke for her. She was trapped inside of herself, longing to feel pretty, accepted, and safe. She was trying to hold it together on the outside, while heartbroken inside. Would it ever not feel like things were falling apart? Would she always need to hide her pain and not believe there really was more to hope for?

But beyond all the food, no matter what size I was, or whether I felt confident about myself or not, there was a much deeper war happening within me. It was the continual plot to destroy the God-given worth that had been spoken over me since before I was born. It went way beyond personal goals or what others said about me or challenges to believe better about myself. Something bigger was stirring in me to want more and actually take the risk to do something about it.

Something bigger was stirring in me to want more and actually take the risk to do something about it.

QUESTIONS AND CHOICES

As I walked through different phases and life experiences, I had to make a choice. My food addiction was real; it was not going away, no matter how hard I tried. It was a secret I didn't want anyone to know about and a burden I kept lugging around with me, not knowing if I could ever stop. One more indulgent binge, hiding wrappers and ice cream cartons to conceal the evidence. How long was I going to keep cycling through the spiral with food binges, secrets, lies, and far-fetched diet plans? I knew something had to change. You can't hide the gluttony of food. Your body mass and cellulite scream out to everyone to take notice. The shame of binge eating screamed louder than everything else.

To say I loved food was a lie. I craved the momentary feeling that food gave me. It was a lust I had let into my life, and I hated everything about it. Something in me felt pleasure and a second of freedom, followed by ongoing shame and guilt. All along, it was a symptom of a bigger problem. For me it was the pain and neglect of not fitting in and the longing for deeper security. I just wanted the internal barrage of criticism to leave and the loneliness to stop.

It was as if God was whispering over and over, "Sandra, put down the food and come to me. You're hungry, but it's not for food. Food has robbed you of so much I have put in you. You want to be seen and noticed and valued; you've been searching for these treasures so you can feel secure and free, but it's not working. Sandra, I see you, and I have what you need. You hold more value than you know. What I have for you goes beyond any formula or body image and invites you to something new, brand new, that you have never experienced before."

I never knew there was more.

Isaiah 43:18–19 (NIV) states, "Forget the former things; do not dwell on the past. See, I am doing a new thing! Now it springs up; do you not perceive it? I am making a way in the desert and streams in the wasteland."

I was entering a new season I knew nothing of yet. Streams in the desert of my soul were closer than I would know.

ONE QUESTION CHANGED EVERYTHING

Towards the end of college, I shifted from my previous career goals to become a doctor and began ministering to teenagers through Young Life, with other leaders and friends who were doing the same. We went on crazy adventures together and spent time laughing, crying, and pouring into others, all with the hopes of them surrendering their lives to God and the transforming work of His Son on their behalf. This passion came after I found myself in the greatest relationship I had ever experienced with a God who had captured my heart and was filling me with His great love and purpose. I felt alive and free; however, I was a work in progress, growing and learning how to lead and influence others amidst the challenges of growing up myself and finding my place. I often still wrestled inside with the emptiness and tried hard to be enough for God, for myself and for others.

As life's path moved me around, I often sat and wondered if I'd ever get married. It was a longing I had wanted but was often afraid to believe it would really happen. After moving back home to complete my nursing degree, I returned to Virginia Beach to start a new life chapter and volunteer with Young Life. While enjoying the rich community of people and trying to adapt to my night shift's sleep schedule, I was set up with a local guy. I knew his brother and wife and was hesitantly optimistic about the opportunity. I had never met him before but decided to give it a chance. What seemed awkward at first then turned into a fast-track friendship, romance, engagement, and marriage. On October 26, 2002, we became Mr. and Mrs. Brett Coates.

Only a short time after getting married, I saw the same patterns of food binges creep in once again. I thought, *Surely by now they were gone?* There I was, standing before my pantry, like so many times before, desperately hoping there wasn't a bag of chocolate chips or some other indulgence hidden somewhere. In those moments, and most other moments, I had no willpower. Just a little bit now and a handful later seemed to be a safe balance and easier to face myself in the mirror. I tried to tell myself not to eat after four, or only put one piece at a time in your mouth, or make sure you divide them into preportioned servings. I would punish myself at meals for my indulgences or feverishly exercise to try and burn off what I had eaten from a lack of self-control. It seemed manageable to me, but I was only fooling myself. When you have a pattern of weaknesses, some might call addiction, you can't just control it yourself. You need something stronger to do more than just shift from overindulging to starving yourself or trying some radical new meal plan.

The war continued on because I had to eat. I used to wish I struggled with something else so I could just stop it all together, but unfortunately, you can't do that with food. Over time, I had completely forgotten who I had been called by God Himself to be, and instead, I settled for so much less. I needed to grasp the fact that the main person in my life struggling with this issue was me. I had been in the pit for too long.

While my ongoing hidden weakness to binge stayed the same, God spoke to me about it. I heard the gentle yet commanding voice while I stood alone in my kitchen, searching for food that I didn't even want. I sighed and said, "Will I always struggle with this?" I wondered what it would be like to not struggle with food and shame behind closed doors. The most powerful question followed, as I heard these words: "Do you want to get well?" I immediately knew this was referring to a powerful story I had read in the Bible many times before.

In John chapter 5, Jesus visits a pool in Jerusalem and sees lots of disabled people. "One who was there had been an invalid for thirty-eight years. When Jesus saw him lying there and learned that he had been in this condition for a long time, he asked him, 'Do you want to get well?'

"'Sir,' the invalid replied, 'I have no one to help me into the pool when the water is stirred. While I am trying to get in, someone else goes down ahead of me.'

"Then Jesus said to him, 'Get up! Pick up your mat and walk.' At once the man was cured: he picked up his mat and walked" (John 5:5, 8 NIV).

Until then, I had never thought about this condition for myself. I never knew there was more. What had I allowed to take over within me and steal what had been given to me? It was my worth, beauty, and purpose, but instead, I felt all the shame, self-loathing, and fear that were magnified and lived within me. For all these years, through all these seasons, I had a real and true identity buried inside that had never seen the light of day. From that day on, I started to get a glimpse of the wellness I was being offered, one desire and one battle at a time.

This was not just a season of despair for me. Like the invalid man, this condition was permanent. Although Jesus may not heal every physical need we have, He does have a plan for that ailment of ours and wants us to experience supernatural healing, the kind of healing you can't help but be forever changed by. It comes as we invite Him to take over and lead us. He gets the praise when His name is glorified and His power is put in its rightful place. Oftentimes, we too can sit waiting by the pool, feeling stuck in our condition. Instead, we can ask our Heavenly Father to get well, made new. The truth is, we have all been given new labels: Chosen, Fought For, Breathtaking, Daughter of the King. These are the titles we were intended to wear because the One who is most worthy gave us these names.

LEAVING ONE BITE

Along this journey of saying yes to God's invitation to getting well, I was shown a different picture of worship. For so long, I had made food an idol to worship, and it was destroying me. As I began this journey, I realized I needed a lot of help. There was so much I had to relearn about food and the power I let it have over me. It was so easy to drift back into old habits. One night, I had a powerful dream that opened my eyes. I was standing in the back of a big room, a sanctuary that was dim but illuminated by a great light. In the front was an altar that commanded this beautiful light source, and I could feel the whole room was filled with reverence. It was my turn to bring something up to the altar as a sacrifice. I felt anxious because I did not feel worthy to bring anything.

The very next moment, I stood in shock as I felt myself walking up to this altar with a used plate in my hands that held the leftover secret dessert I had been eating. There was one bite left, and instead of eating it myself, I saw that it wasn't for me. Instead, this seemingly unimportant piece of food suddenly became my offering. It was as if I was saying, "God, You are more important than this food."

In that moment, I was flooded with a clarity I had never known before. This sweet, sinful indulgence no longer had a hold on me, and my Lord was now my worship. He was my sweet indulgence, far greater than any tempting food. It was the greatest movement of being made new in the backdrop of having no self-control and being mastered by food. Gluttony and shame had turned into breathtaking worship. I was no longer a slave to this glaring sin. He was the One who satisfied my appetite, down to the deepest parts I didn't even understand. He was my rescue story.

Psalm 145:16 (NIV) says, "You open your hand and satisfy the desires of every living thing."

As I began to learn how to navigate life with food in its appropriate place of nourishment, "Do not handle, do not taste, do not touch" (Colossians 2:21 NIV) became my scripture mantra over the food that tried to control me or lure me into its temporary delicacies. I'd love to tell you that it was quick and painless, and I got it right the first hundred times, but that is far from the truth. It was the slow death of a comfortable lover that had been enticing me as far back as I can remember. It was repenting after thinking I could have trigger foods in my house to tempt me. It was learning not to buy sweet things that I kind of liked because I couldn't trust myself. It was God's patience with me, teaching me that it was He who set out on a rescue mission to set me free. I couldn't believe He had chosen me and my hidden and shameful addiction to food.

"Open wide your mouth and I will fill it, declares the Lord" (Psalm 81:10 NIV). This declaration is one of the most mind-blowing statements. If you take hold of what it says and actually let God fill you with His absolute goodness, instead of continually trying to fill the void yourself, your life will be nothing short of miraculous. I am living proof of that.

As I started to taste the pleasure of having the willpower to actually say no to food when my body said otherwise, I felt a rush of fullness and new strength I have never felt before. What was impossible to pass up wherever trigger food was, now began to stir in me to see something bigger, something past all the familiar temptations. Self-control had been a foreign concept in my everyday life and one I had only prayed for at a distance. I would get envious of others who seemed to live a life of routine, balance, and had joy doing it. I was always one who would start something with great intentions, but as quickly as I started I would lose interest because the assignment did not seem worth all the work and discipline involved.

With food, the denial became so much more pleasurable than the indulgence. I don't honestly know all that happened, but I know it is something crazy, something more powerful and specific to me. In her book *Gay Girl, Good God*, Jackie Hill Perry writes, "Before I knew it, I was back, with the same temptation and with someone else's power." As I surrendered myself more, I saw more of God's power over my desire to binge eat. Because let's be real: Cinnamon buns covered in cream cheese icing, a favorite box of Girl Scout cookies, ice cream, or dark chocolate anything was like kryptonite to me without any limits. All the food goals for that particular day were nowhere in sight.

For me, the battle was with food, but there are so many things that we can allow to control our lives. Perhaps the pills that started out as pain relief are now something you can't function without. Maybe you once enjoyed a glass of wine or an occasional cocktail, but now you can't control how many you drink. Or the fun, innocent flirting that turns into lust or seduction because you were longing to connect with someone for attention. In those moments of need, our moral standards seem to disappear, and we can so quickly do the very things we don't want to do.

The apostle Paul spoke of this struggle with sin. He writes, "I do not understand what I do. For what I do is not the good I want to do; no, the evil I do not want to do—this I keep on doing. For in my inner being I delight in God's law; but I see another law at work in the members of my body, waging war against the law of my mind and making me a prisoner of the law of sin" (Romans 7:15b, 19, 22 – 23 NIV).

This is not the end of the story. We are in a battle far greater than what we ourselves can overcome.

To my fellow sisters, who are trying so hard to be OK when the rejection and shame and emptiness speak so loud, and you're more comfortable being on the run or in hiding; for those who put up brick walls so no one can enter into your heart; and for those who appear with an commanding presence in hopes of scaring everyone away, know that you are seen, and so is your weariness. Deep within, your wounded heart and battle marks have been noted. The One Who sees is the same One Who created you for a great kingdom purpose. The Bible says God works all things together for good. Romans 8:28a (NIV) says, "Only He sees it all and has the power to make something so good out of it."

Our destiny will always be bigger than our circumstances, but first we need to face the war at hand. I had to face the giant that told me I wasn't enough, and I would never be enough. It spun me around in cycles of shame, insecurity, and fear, leaving me gasping for air. On the

> **I had to face the giant that told me I wasn't enough, and I would never be enough.**

outside, I worked hard to keep things looking as normal as I could because I wanted to believe they were.

There wasn't anything man made that could heal me. The only remedy was going to be that which seemed impossible to my human mind. It would be my life story as a testimony to the very power of the One Who commanded "the winds and the waves to obey Him" (Matthew 8:27 NIV). And they did.

When I looked in the mirror, I often got sidetracked as I ran through the critical thoughts about myself and my many stretch marks. I realized all the miracle creams or programs were not going to work; these marks would be embedded in my skin forever. These marks represented deeper reminders of labels I couldn't deny weren't the truth. The sabotaging and familiar questions often came flooding back: "Why did I have to grow so fast as a kid? Eat so much? Be so big? Feel so terrible every time I saw myself in a swimsuit? Why did I care so much about what others thought?" I was craving something new out of things I myself could do nothing to change. I felt ongoing attacks, not only on my self-image and my beauty, but my identity. I never knew I wasn't the only one listening. "You have searched me, Lord, and you know me. Before a word is on my tongue you, Lord, know it completely" (Psalm 139:1, 4 NIV).

The epiphany came after I was talking with a close friend who remarked about her stretch marks. They reminded her of being pregnant and the joy it brought that she could bear children. In my head, I was confused; could such permanent marks actually be something noble and produce something good? I had never thought of it that way. I was too busy being held in a state of condemnation over mine. As I resonated with her as another member of the "stretch mark club," I realized maybe there was another meaning, a hidden treasure there for me too. It was out of her great perspective that I found those same marks told a battle story of my life too. It was in the secret place that they reminded me of a God who rescued me from condemnation and defeat. He instead was making me into a warrior, one who would not run on her own strength but out of His power and victory placed within her.

"Praise be to the Lord, my Rock, who trains my hands for war, my fingers for battle. He is my loving God and my fortress, my stronghold and my deliverer, my shield in whom I take refuge, who subdues peoples under me" (Psalm 144:1–2 NIV).

BUILDING THE WARRIOR

God rewrote my self-worth and ultimately my identity. It took time for me to see and believe there was more for me, my purpose, and my life. It took the gracious and overwhelming love of the Father to accomplish this. For so long, I had been living in defeat of the labels and disappointments, as well as repeating cycles that seemed to always end with me questioning myself. There were thin layers of strength and drive that I tried to use to compensate for the internal attacks in my head, but none of them proved to last. Ultimately, it was His great and relentless love for me to know Him through this new identity. My insecure body image, ongoing wounds, and critical self talk got to come with me on this new journey, but no longer did they define me or dictate my value. A greater work had been done in me, where for the first time, I could start to see myself through a grander lens, one that called me radiant, fully accepted, and beautiful, just as I was. I began to discover that I had been a warrior in training this whole time: the adversity of my childhood, being ostracized and questioned for my size, and the struggle with food were all part of it. I had scars from life's battles, many unseen, but they were being used to cultivate a new strength rather than tear down the little strength I carried with me.

It was never about food. It was really the war tactic against the glorious identity I had been appointed to know about. For me, food happened to fit the bill. The method was to keep me in a state of condemnation, feeling defeated and unstable, believing I had to measure up and keep working to earn the little worth I could see. I was starting to see the effects of God's healing in me and wanted to become the warrior He designed me to be. There would still be more battles to walk through in my journey ahead.

OUT OF CONTROL

My husband Brett and I have three amazing sons. In September of 2013, our youngest son was born. His birth followed a fast and furious rush to the hospital after waking up in pain, which quickly announced what was ahead. I had been hustling hard just like I always did with each of my pregnancies, working as a nurse up until the very end while chasing my two boys everywhere. My body was slowing down, and my feet were swelling up earlier and earlier each day. I had plans for this birth and was looking forward to a peaceful delivery, complete with a glorious epidural like I had with the other two. I was never that interested in all-natural birthing options. I listened with narrowed eyes as my older sister and close friends told of these heroic birth plans and stories of their superhero powers. I gladly resolved that I was not given those same superpowers and was A-OK to not have this as part of my life story. In fact, I got pretty anxious about the thought of not feeling control over my body and the pain that would take place once labor got going. Natural or not, it was not an experience I needed or wanted.

The contractions started in the wee hours of the morning and didn't let up. I realized in my slumber the familiar pains of labor were back, albeit spread out, but not going away. I don't know why I thought I could make it a little longer, but each time I was awakened by a contraction, I told myself I could go back to sleep. The same thing happened again and again throughout the darkness of the early morning, until my body made it clear it was time to head to the hospital. I told Brett about the overnight events, stopping to breathe through my pain in a rhythmic pattern. His eyes got big, and he quickly changed to go-mode. As we rushed to the car and texted our neighbor to come over, I realized the situation was not what I had planned. The whole way there, the sinking feeling set in as I told myself, *I'm too late for an epidural.*

We raced into the labor and delivery unit, and all I could remember was Brett asking the young girl who checked us in if she could get the epidural ready, to which she responded, "Sir, I don't make those decisions, but they will be right with you."

That morning, the beds were completely full on the unit, and the triage nurse was more than ready for her change of shift from the previous night. My nine-centimeter dilation was not the news she wanted, as I now writhed in the bed, trying to breathe. I got into a room and was checked in with an official bracelet; they told me I was ten centimeters, and it was, in fact, too late for an epidural. I heard what they said but could not accept it and was trying every angle to get around that fate. I was in so much pain but did not realize what was coming next. The labor and delivery nurse got really close to me and told me they were going to break my water so I could start pushing, but I needed to follow her directions closely.

What she meant to say was, this is going to be the worst pain in your life, so get ready. After that point, all I remember is I screamed so loud I lost my voice. Think screams out of a murder scene (according to my husband), with two doctors and about six nurses all rushing into the room at once. I pushed and screamed and tried to find a place to focus, but there just wasn't one. After fifteen minutes, the most darling and handsome boy who had just wreaked all that havoc was born and laid peacefully on my chest.

As wild of a story as that is, deep down, his birth sent me into a state of anxiety and triggered some deeper trauma. I was now home with two young boys and a newborn. I felt robbed of the birth experience I had imagined and was not at all ready to cope with what was happening. My oldest son had just been diagnosed with high functioning autism, with no medical treatment in sight. We were navigating daily how to parent him and figure out his needs and our expectations. My middle son had just started preschool and routinely had to be pried away from me as we approached his classroom. I would cry after I dropped him off because I, too, aligned with his precious heart of not wanting to fly the coop. My new baby was adjusting to breastfeeding and sleep schedules, and I was on duty as a mom of three all hours of the day and night. Brett, who was giving all he had to us, was maneuvering a brand-new season as an executive pastor while also having to fill the shoes of the church after a sudden loss of our lead pastor.

I wanted so badly to keep up with everything and make those around me happy, but the toll it took on me grew quickly. I tried to perform all the duties, but there were so many needs that I couldn't fill, namely to take care of me. I told myself that it was just a phase, coupled with unbalanced hormones, and all would be OK as each day passed. As the days and weeks passed, the reminders that I was not in control of my time, my schedule, or my body started to sink in. This felt like my permanent reality, not just a season of practices and recitals for the big show. I went back to work part time as a nurse; I enjoyed helping others and getting a break from my role at home. I could go to the bathroom when I needed, sit and quietly work at the computer, or meet with patients where there were no interruptions.

It was a great reprieve, and I was a better mom for it. I would speak of the adorableness of my new babe and all the blessings we now had as a healthy family of five. If I'm honest, I was really talking about what I would have liked to believe and about what I thought of my husband and my three young boys, but not of myself. I had forgone my own health for the sake of my family and was about to pay an even bigger price for it all. As a pastor's wife connected in my church and community, I wanted to keep up with the pace that life brought and the expectations surrounding me. I tried to fight back the loneliness and fatigue while still giving to others. Despite my inner life feeling like it was caving in, I still tried everything in my own power to handle the days and keep up with what I saw as being strong. Meanwhile, all I wanted to do was get off the crazy ride that kept spinning in circles.

Fast-forward a few weeks; the Thanksgiving holidays were approaching. I kept moving as hard and as fast as I could, soaking in the moments that were so precious amidst the sea of tasks and constant interruptions. Friends and medical professionals would offer advice and try to help me work towards a better home schedule to get some respite. I wanted to succeed so badly and get out of the cycle of feeling stuck and defeated, but it always seemed to fall short. Every day, it felt like I was barraged by the mental attacks. It felt empowering to be reassured by other moms who had gone before me and offered their secret plans, but to carry it out seemed as if I always came up way short.

The baby still couldn't get comfortable away from my arms, and every time I tried a new schedule, I felt defeat breathing down my neck. I began seeing the episodes of panic encroaching as I started losing more and more confidence in my decisions. Self-sabotage and stress dominated my thought patterns. There was no beauty here, or so I thought. I often found myself comparing things to other new moms, who seemed blissful with their babies, who appeared perfectly rested and on a great schedule. *I should know how to do this*, I often thought to myself. I've already had two babies, and boys at that, so this should be easy, right? I grew harder on myself and would still say yes to hosting people for dinner at our house, when inside

I knew I could barely hold on. I was spiraling down, but there was neither time nor space to attend to my cries for help, so they remained silent.

By December of that year, I was rushing around, getting ready for work, when Brett asked me a simple question about the day's feeding schedule for the baby. I started panicking, burst into tears, and shouted, "I don't know!" As he tried to clarify and ask questions to trace back the overnight hours and feedings, my head started spinning, and I couldn't breathe. I wasn't sure if the last time I was up with him was for eating, a diaper change, or something else.

At that moment, the level of anxiety I felt hit a new level. All I saw and felt was failure. From there, I tried to recover as best I could, but it wasn't going away. I began to have panic attacks and asked Brett to work from home just so I wouldn't feel so alone. The following Monday, I ended up at the doctor's office, pleading for help. They took my blood and had me fill out a questionnaire about my emotional well-being. I answered yes to basically everything and was fed up with the defeat and tears I had tried to fend off.

My doctor sat down to tell me my results.

"You have no immune system right now," she began, "and you're completely overwhelmed. You need sleep; you need to take a break from all your responsibilities and watch funny movies and laugh. Maybe a weekend getaway? Can you do that?"

I looked at her with dark circles under my eyes and a somber, pale face. I held back the sarcasm and said, as graciously as I could, "That's kind of impossible to do right now."

I began to tell her how I was locked into all these responsibilities and all the people who depended on me. She listened and challenged me to ask for help, as she could tell I had been trying to be all things to all people.

She prescribed some medicine for anxiety and depression, and I took my frail and weathered self home. It would be the beginning of a climb God would take me on, out of the pit I had fallen into, one day at a time.

A year later, I reflected on those roller-coaster days and wrote this is my journal:

> It is so good to look back and see that I was not alone. I'm realizing the Lord was uncovering things I was believing that are just not true and not mine to carry. I am thankful for coming to the end of myself and sobbing all the way home after work. Feeling so scared, incapable, insecure, and unstable, I cried out to You [God] and surrendered it all. Through cries and pleas, my prayers turned into praises and proclamations of Truth. Something lifted in me. My spirit was free again, and I could be me. LORD, I thank you for Your great strength and love over me. I have learned that anxiety has been a part of my life since I was a little girl. But YOU are working in and through me to replace all that panic with power. I don't have to take on the stress around me. It is not my battle to fight. Father, teach me how to do this, to not be rattled by bad news or ups and downs of life or let emotions dictate me. Secure my footing of who I am and who I belong to.

What I didn't know during that taxing season was that one season didn't tell my story or dictate my efforts as a mom or a wife or a woman. There was a God who was interceding on my behalf, fighting for me, my children, and my marriage the whole time. He was carrying us through the uncharted messy days and crafting something unbelievably great.

Exodus 14:14 (NLT) says, "The Lord himself will fight for you. Just stay calm."

| NOT FORGOTTEN

In this life, it's often hard to find your place, that sacred place where you feel like you can thrive and truly be yourself. As I look back at the areas of life that provided deep, lasting satisfaction, they all came from one place: me accepting an invitation to be my fully exposed and messed-up self before a perfect God. Now, getting there meant coming to the end of myself and all my efforts to hide the mess. It also meant casting away my own formulas for what I deemed a success that left me falling short every time. As I allowed God to come into my life and ask the hard and deep questions, He began to do His work. The more I offered Him the open cracks in me—the flaws, the aching desires, the scars, and the fresh wounds of life—He brought me deeper. I realized I needed a power source bigger than me, one I didn't have to start at the beginning to explain myself to, one that crafted every line on my hands and feet, knew me all along, and reminded me who I was and who I wasn't. It felt good to want to come out of hiding.

"Ah, Sovereign Lord, you have made the heavens and the earth by your great power and outstretched arm. Nothing is too hard for you" (Jeremiah 32:17 NIV).

This verse sits on an index card above my kitchen sink next to a favorite picture of Brett and my boys, all in matching outfits. The card is sprinkled with water stains and wrinkles, and the words are now faded. I am reminded of the blissful moments in time witnessed from that special photo. But what about all the before-and-after moments: the struggles, the doubts, the noise, the fear, and chaos? How many times have I stood there and wondered if the giant, ugly, hard thing I am facing in my life will ever feel smaller than my faith? What about the ongoing battles of marriage, parenting, feeling inadequate, and longing for a glimmer of hope? What about my longing for a little girl? *Ouch.* That one sunk deep. It was costly to hope in something I only dreamed of from a distance. It was a bond I longed for, but it did not come.

Though we have not been forgotten, we may find ourselves in that mindset. This is a long-standing tactic the enemy uses to have us try and find our own way. If he can distract us from believing there is already a glorious plan of victory marked out for us, just as we are, then he has done his job.

Every woman and every girl longs to be noticed, to have someone want to rescue her because she is desired and special. They want to take someone's breath away because of their beauty. Why do we save love notes and fill our phones with moments we want to hold forever and watch Hallmark movies (even though we know how they end)? Because every woman, young and old, wants to be called the one. The secret is discovering that her name already has been called by God, the One Who deems her worthy.

It can be easy to fall into the trap and believe you know the end of your story or the situation you find yourself in. So often, we don't even realize our shortsightedness. But what if God is using every scrap of your life to bring you to a new place, with a new hope and a new anticipation of how He will rewrite your story? He really wants your angst, your depression, your suicidal thoughts, and all your reasons why it feels so scary to believe there really is more than what you have seen. Jesus simply but boldly declares, "I have come that they may have life and have it to the full" (John 10:10 NIV).

> **But what if God is using every scrap of your life to bring you to a new place, with a new hope and a new anticipation of how He will rewrite your story?**

You can't make something out of nothing. I had nothing in my favor. I was at the end of me but deep down still wanted more. There wasn't a playbook, a formula, or a role model with my same history, my scars, and my deep-seated fear of rejection. My gene pool was not helping me; both my parents struggled with their weight. I very often heard the line "I'm sorry you were not blessed with good genes." But You, oh God, tell me it's never too late, I'm never too flawed, too far gone, or too rejected. He makes something great out of my nothing.

What really happened was this: when I thought I was left, I was actually found. When I thought no one saw me, He made Himself known. When I thought my beauty and purpose were nowhere in sight, He showed me they had been there from the beginning. In my cries over all that I was not, His sweet whisper of new promise showed me not one tear was missed. He had held my heart the whole way and it was safe. I was not forgotten. Ever.

"I will see the goodness of the Lord in the land of the living. Wait for the Lord; be strong and take heart and wait for the Lord" (Psalm 27:13–14 NIV).

MADE ON PURPOSE (SCARS AND ALL)

It often blows my mind that God decided to take me on and show me His beauty within me. He took me from begging to be someone different (more dainty, more confident, and more secure) to a brave and scarred woman who others want to follow and marvel at my poise and confidence. None of it is mine. I spent many seasons of my life in the wrestling ring, fighting with my little girl strength and flimsy homemade weapons. But when God stepped in, and I

> **I spent many seasons of my life in the wrestling ring, fighting with my little girl strength and flimsy homemade weapons.**

said yes, it all changed. The stretch marks didn't have any more accusations, and the measuring stick of perfection no longer stood before me. The wounds of rejection from those who said I was disqualified began to heal.

Like being underwater and desperately trying to reach surface, where it's light and there is air to breathe, I now understood I was just as chosen as any other girl, even though my pain and my wounds were still so real. God was wiring me to be a living testimony of the very thing I longed for. He was the Warrior Who was fighting my battles and setting me free.

The Bible tells us to hold every thought captive and to be transformed by the renewing of our mind. Is there really a war? Yes- There is an enemy who targets his strategy against women knowing their value and worth. Our God delights in us. He is enthralled by us. We belong to this perfect, and holy, heavenly gentleman. But if we try to find value on our own, what happens? In short, it doesn't work. We may use worldly methods to uphold our value, but those methods are temporary, weak, and often self-focused. Once we can see our worth through Christ, look out. When we see the gift we are to God, to our loved ones, and to this world, we start to exude joy, peace, security, strength, and self-care. We say no to pleasing everyone; we stop compromising ourselves to make others happy.

One day, I was checking out at the grocery store when I noticed the cashier's arms. Normally, I don't look down because I'm too busy getting my items out of the cart. But I couldn't help noticing the perfectly spaced-out cuts lining her forearms. They were scarred over and looked different from the rest of her skin. She was a beautiful young girl with a warm smile and friendly demeanor. My thoughts immediately went to wonder why such a vibrant young woman would cut herself. I knew each mark held a story and represented a time in her life where something was dark or painful, or maybe she just felt numb.

I wanted to tell her I saw her beauty; I wanted to remind her she was amazing, despite whatever she'd been through. She finished my grocery order, and I wheeled away the cart; we never got to have that conversation. After I walked out of the store and went on my way, I still wondered about her. What drove her need to cut herself and leave permanent marks on her body? Was it a release of pain? A cry for help, or a welcomed release to feel something? Maybe it was boredom or loneliness.

We all have a story, and I wanted to know hers, but I didn't get to that day. It was unlike anyone else's. She, like me and so many others, shares in the marks of our scars. Jesus, the Savior of the world, is known for His scars. He is the very One Who redeems our scars and our pain, whatever they look like. The Bible speaks of this very truth: "He himself bore our sins in his body on the cross, so that we might die to sins and live for righteousness; by his wounds you have been healed" (1 Peter 2:24 NIV).

Don't be afraid of your weaknesses, your messes, or your failures; God can handle those. As we see over and over in scripture, He actually speaks the loudest when we stand before Him broken, weak, and unable to fix ourselves but longing for more. There is no magic formula to confidence or success. You can have all the goals in life, coaches and business plans and secrets to the top, and still fall short. What happens in life is, when things fall apart, it becomes clearer. It is often in the chasm between the uncomfortable spaces and the desperate places that we are offered to see things differently. The view we hold is a human one with rational conclusions based on facts, experiences, and abilities. The challenge for us may be admitting we are still thirsty and the water we ourselves have to drink is not enough. We must not give up searching.

▌LONGING FOR BEAUTY

In Matthew 11:28 (NIV), Jesus says, "Come to Me all who are weary and burdened, and I will give you rest." If you want to be free from the invisible chains that hold you down, fantastic, but it will require some discomfort: surrender. We simply have to be at the end of ourselves and longing for something new; we must want more than what we can think or imagine. We have to want to get well and be set free. The greatest gift I've seen in my personal development came out of surrender in the hardest places. I had to be willing to ask the difficult questions. It's this recognition: "OK, God, I'm desperate. No more formulas, no more personality tests, no more advice from peers and bosses and parents. I need to know there is a place and a journey set out just for me, and it has been there since the beginning. A plan that uses the very nature of me and all of my crazy, complicated self to come fully alive, not empty and restlessly still searching." Oh, to risk looking like a failure in exchange for feeling fully alive, exactly where I was; this was a risk I was willing to take. In her book *Uninvited*, Lysa TerKeurst says it simply and powerfully: "The more fully we invite God in, the less we will feel uninvited by others."

My journey ahead discovering beauty and having it emerge was never about me becoming successful or in the spotlight. It was, however, about a transformation and a platform emerging for something far greater. It was where my heart burst forth to want every woman of every age, race, size, and culture to experience the unspeakable treasure of her God-given beauty through her story. It is for us all to experience the richness of God's healing as He takes us down to the roots of where we first hid in shame, feeling guilty and thinking we had not achieved enough. These are the chains that keep us bound, and this is where the breakthrough starts. "The greatest spiritual battle of our generation is being fought between our ears. This is the epicenter of the battle" (Jennie Allen, *Get Out of Your Head*).

THE GREAT REVERSAL (MODELING JOURNEY)

Being a wife, mom, part-time nurse, and women's ministry leader kept me quite busy, but I was still restless. I worked for a number of years at a pregnancy medical clinic, performing ultrasounds and speaking to young women in crisis. It challenged me and taught me to look at my own self, struggles and all; I wondered if there was more. In this season, I was missing excitement and new endeavors, apart from my world of diapers and nap times, hosting parties, and pouring into others. I needed my own outlet, to dream again and just be a girl. Even though I was all grown up, the labels still sunk deep. The questions about my size and my height were still buried deep inside. Will the ache for more ever leave? Could I get up the guts to try something far beyond my reach?

I had always dreamed of becoming a model, to use my height to my advantage; I thought I'd arrive at finding the beauty label if I achieved that title. The problem was, I never liked people looking at me; there was always a risk of what they were thinking and saying about me. I was conditioned to stay guarded and uncomfortable in these situations, as I stood out like a sore thumb. I decided to give it a try, despite my insecurity.

I called a local modeling agency and met with a woman from the agency. I got headshots made, attended classes, and started getting a taste of this world. I realized there were lots of beautiful faces and lots of competition. The industry was about showing off confidence and making clothes and brands look their best. At a charity fashion show, I quickly realized I was not cut out for this. I didn't have anything to wear in the show until the last minute, when one of the seasoned models felt bad and gave me an extra dress of hers. It was not a magical moment, walking the runway and trying to put on a smile. It wasn't a good fit for me. I lacked confidence, and it showed. I didn't see the value in it. I realized I was really looking for something more, but it didn't exist. I needed a community of ladies who together could build one another up for a greater purpose than themselves and do something fun and creative at the same time. I had no idea that something like this existed until years later, when I embarked on a new journey that would change me forever.

At the end of 2016, I heard these words deep within me: *I have an opportunity for you.* I had been encouraged to pursue modeling and speaking on a more professional level but never felt like I had what it took. Anytime I thought that way, the list of disqualifications would take their stabs at me. *Who do you think you are?* This script played over and over in my mind. When you study the best and the most polished in the field, you can suddenly feel like a fool in comparison.

After I got up the courage to tell a few trusted people about it, I took a leap again and auditioned with Actors, Models & Talent for Christ (AMTC), a nationwide Christian talent agency. More than any talent, I wanted to grow in my stage presence; I wanted to be a mature runway model, perhaps using my nursing experience. With hesitation and some legit fear, I met a scouting agent online and gave it my best. I learned what a monologue was and prepared a speech from what I knew: working with women in unplanned pregnancies. I played myself, a nurse, and offered a dramatic scene of working with a patient who believed she was pregnant. After the awkward silence and standard feedback ("Thank you for your time, you will hear from us soon"), I embraced the mentality of learning from my mistakes, since it all felt really uncomfortable.

However, later, an email arrived, telling me I was accepted and would train as an actress and model; I couldn't believe it.

With Brett on board, and after many sacrifices, I started going into New York City for training. It was a wonderful time and also very challenging, which was something I had missed. I was out of my comfort zone and needed to take inventory of who I was and who I represented on stage. Every talented performer in the program had a unique look. It was amazing. I met the most incredible people, and I got to spend days with my mom and stepmom, bonding over our NYC trips. I learned some great principles about creativity, potential, and the value of every person God has made. There is no one else like them. Better yet, He wants to use each and every unique talent as a tool to reach the world for His kingdom.

I launched my journey of saying yes to God in the entertainment industry. It was scary and uncomfortable, and I often couldn't see past my less-than-perfect body, lack of confidence, and clumsiness. You have to be good at taking criticism and rejection to seek out new opportunities when you are in the talent world. I realized we often live in a bubble of safe environments and miss the great opportunities to be light and salt in a desperate and lonely world. Being called to share the love of Jesus with others is a privilege. There may be more talented people in this world, but God appoints us to go on a specific and unique journey. The places He calls us to may be uncomfortable and often downright scary, but they draw out insecurities so we can complete the work He calls us to. These experiences prune us and strip us down to be firmly rooted with new potential to grow again. Through it all, He does the greater work in us, as we remain rooted in Him and the glorious kingdom of heaven grows.

I began to realize God's place in my life had shown through to the outside, and He wanted me to stand out once again among the world. But this time, it was different. No longer was I to hide my size and my height, but rather expose who I was all along, with the beauty that came with it. This was the great reversal of my size and stature. This time, I was needed for just who I was, without apology, nothing more, nothing less. He was making "beauty from ashes" and doing the unthinkable by taking me from the pit of my mess and insecurity to living a testimony of a beautiful rescue. I started getting more and more compliments about my beauty and confidence.

Being in the spotlight had forever been a place of danger, where comments and ridicule flowed freely. What started as uncomfortable and awkward to receive became a sign of His elegant handiwork and testimony in me.

| TAKING THE PLUNGE

I was standing in line at a casting call for an upcoming fashion show. There were so many girls lined up to compete for a few spots in the show. You could see them looking up and down and all around, sizing up who might be the greatest competition. We were all dressed alike: black tights, fitted black tank top, and black heels, waiting for our turn to walk in front of the judges. As I looked around at the sea of perfectly shaped bodies, beautiful faces, and confident women, my mind was screaming, *Why are you even here?*

When it was my turn, I put on my best pose and pretended I was among the elite, while everything in me wanted to run out. After everyone auditioned, we waited to see who made the show. I had my duffle bag in hand, coat on, ready to leave. To my disbelief, I heard my number and my name called. I looked around to see if someone else had my name and then sheepishly raised my hand. There must have been some mistake, but there wasn't.

I gathered with the other ladies to get fitted for Chico's fashion collection; everything had shifted quickly. I had assumed one thing, rejection, but instead, I got the opposite: chosen to be here. As the music started and we lined up to showcase the new designs, I realized it's good to take a chance and try something out of your comfort zone, even if you think you don't qualify.

It was a good day to see another side of me. God was rewriting my story and teaching me to stop running away from opportunities, despite the potential for rejection. What if He had decided that I should be His vessel that day? Whether on or off the runway, how many other women around me needed to know their beauty?

When that day was over, I realized God used every situation, and I may never know the reason why, so I straightened myself up a little higher. This was for me, but not just for me. It was about her, and her, and her. As the models all said our goodbyes and went our separate ways, I was grateful to have made some new friends that day. But even bigger, I realized I was a piece of a rescue mission straight from the heart of a God who never stops pursuing His daughters and saying they are worth far greater than the world could ever see.

The following spring, there was another show; I auditioned again, wearing my shiny black heels backstage in preparation for the rehearsal. Again dressed in black fitted tanks and leggings, the ladies got lined up and ready to walk out for the show's producer. It was an international fashion show with models and designers from around the world. For the first time, I was not the tallest woman there, but rather one among many. The difference between us was, they overflowed with confidence and appeared effortless on the runway, while I felt every ounce of insecurity and pressure to perform better. I studied their postures and intently watched their practice walks for a quick refresher on what I was supposed to be doing. Why was I here again?

Somehow, all the time I practiced felt like a lifetime ago; I was not qualified to be there. I put on a calm smile and tried my best to act confident. I was among elite models, both local and international. They were amazing to watch and learn from. The ongoing battle was believing in myself, knowing that I belonged there, despite feeling unqualified and uncomfortable.

God whispered, "You're right; you don't fit in. I've called you out of your comfort zone to be a reflection of my light. Love others with the love I've shown you, the kind that wants nothing in return but to value who they really are."

I realized I had to focus on the beauty within me. I didn't need to be in a fashion show to learn that, but God used this experience to show me the satisfying treasure He is in me and how He wants to pour that out onto others. For every girl around me, my heart burst at the seams to show this powerful beauty that radiates from God. Every woman needed to know she's breathtaking.

Later, I joined the Christian Modeling Association (CMA), a group that encouraged women of faith how to act and believe as part of the modeling world. It was so helpful to know that I could be in a community of other women who wanted to honor God in the modeling industry and hold a high standard to stand out for His glory.

One day, in a complete surprise, my headshot appeared on her Instagram post. I was being featured on her site under the label of "GODFIDENCE." I was speechless to be featured on her site, especially because the very thing I lacked the most and wanted so badly in my life was confidence. Even though it was only a social media post nestled in with so many millions of others, it challenged me to believe in myself more. God's confidence had broken through in me. It wouldn't be mine to just hold on to, but rather to give away. Oh, the great reversal of God, Who is always working on our behalf.

"Those who look to the Lord are radiant, their faces are never covered with shame" (Psalm 34:5 NIV).

Our true calling on this earth is not about making us a better, more polished version of ourselves. It is rather to encounter the breathtaking, pure love from God Himself, just for us. Out of this transformation, we are emptied of ourselves and made into the image of Jesus Christ, Who removes our sin and the shame that says that we are not good enough, pretty enough, or talented enough. He came to this earth specifically to show you and I who we are and have always been, marked with a beauty that is far bigger than us.

> **He came to this earth specifically to show you and I who we are and have always been, marked with a beauty that is far bigger than us.**

As I look back, the very thing I wanted came forth through the battle of defeat. I was convinced that fear and insecurity and ongoing shame would have the last word. Food and clothing sizes were left behind like vapor, compared to the new platform I stood on. There was no going back, and I now understood food, appearance, and numbers on a scale paled in comparison. God had me on a journey of being looked at, stared at, once again. This time, it was brand new, and it would become the very thing that breathed life into me. I wanted every girl to feel that. The end goal for me is not that I gained confidence or started doing modeling, but rather, the transformed work He had done in me would radiate out of me for His kingdom purpose. His timeless and perfect beauty would soon stretch farther than I could ever imagine. But first, there would be training and preparation.

Reflection/Discussion

What about Your Story?

Reflection: Take some time to write out your unique story, including battles, wounds, and scars. If this feels overwhelming, use the template provided below to generate ideas:

All I ever wanted to be was_____. Instead, I was dealt with _____. All I see is_____. The hardest things for me to believe about myself are ____.

What voices speak the loudest?
Who are the biggest influences in your life?
What does the world tell you, you should be? What do family, friends, and social media tell you?

Exercise: Ask yourself the following questions:

What do you hear yourself saying about you (it might be when you see yourself in front of a mirror or what someone else said)?
You say/hear_____.
What did that make you believe about yourself?

Truth: There may be ongoing reminders that your life story has already been written, and you may feel stuck. You may like you've gone too far. But it's not the end.

If you were to believe what God says about you, what do you imagine you would hear yourself saying about you? (Use these scriptures to guide you: Philippians 1:6; Isaiah 43:1–4, 18–19; Lamentations 3:22–23; Ephesians 2:10.)

Big Idea: We can't change our DNA or the painful parts in our lives, but we get to choose what voices we are going to believe and who has the final say. God wants to take these areas of greatest struggle in your life and do miraculous things.

"Who is this coming up from the wilderness leaning on her beloved?" (Song of Songs 8:5 NIV). God tells us we get to lean on Him rather than find our way alone.

Go back and add what you are now claiming as your new story. (Journal your thoughts or write a prayer to God.)

PART 2

Inside the War

> To be prepared for war is one of the most
> effective means of preserving peace.
> —George Washington

As women who have been created with a purpose, to bear God's image and hold a piece of His beauty, we must know there will be opposition. It may not be a full-on physical war that we think of, but make no mistake; tensions, strongholds, and opposing forces will be all around us, and there will be battle wounds to prove it.

In 1 Peter 5:8 (NIV), we are warned of this: "Be alert and sober minded. Your enemy the devil prowls around like a roaring lion looking for someone to devour." We don't have to look very far to know this to be true. When we realize that war is at hand and live out of our God-given identity instead of our own, we will hold a strength and beauty that is capable of slaying giants. We will be part of the greatest force for good there is. It will grow in power as those who are being set free grow in number.

On the other hand, if we become distracted and deceived into not knowing who we really are and believing we need to find our own way out, the never-ending fight will continue within ourselves. We will seek to confuse and destroy one another. This is the ultimate strategy of the evil one, who knows these tactics are perhaps his greatest path of victory.

"For we wrestle not against flesh and blood, but against principalities, against powers, against the rulers of the darkness of this world, against spiritual wickedness in high places" (Ephesians 6:12a KJV).

We will need weapons: shields of faith, swords, and armor to protect us from our enemy. Our biggest weapons will begin within our minds, by seeking, knowing, and living out what is truth. It will be here, with God's strength and favor, that we stand victoriously behind the great warriors who have gone before us. The result is a growing army of women and girls, fighting together on one another's behalf.

Note: There are many battle analogies to choose from and many more tactics lurking to come against us. The ones discussed below happen to be those I have seen in my own life and those around me.(Comparison, Confidence, Compromise, Control)

COMPARISON

Merriam-Webster Dictionary defines *comparison* as "The act of examining things to see if they are similar or different: the condition of being examined to find similarity or difference."

It begins with a thought we never intended would lead to more. As a society, we are groomed to believe that we have to somehow keep working for the roles we play and the approval we crave. We are taught that if we do anything less, we are lacking. The danger comes when the voices outside beckon us to take charge of ourselves and follow the mindset of the world. We have been deceived into thinking that we must keep striving, keep setting more goals, and keep building an empire of influence.

No one would say that comparison, in and of itself, is bad. It is rather what we compare ourselves to that can either motivate us to do better, or exhaust us and make us feel worse. Comparison can block us from wanting to be made new by the very beauty and strength of God available in us. Deep down, we all are wired to crave more than what we can see and experience. After a while, we don't know what to do with the letdowns, pains, and scars of this life. There are questions deep down that just cannot be satisfied, unless we take our eyes off ourselves. To do that, we must stop comparing ourselves to others. Instead, what if we loosened our grip, surrendered our minds, and gave it all to God Almighty? Ultimately we all have a choice: to cling to His words or ours.

NO LONGER A THREAT

There will always be someone more beautiful, more talented, and with more experience than you, and living the life you wish you had. It can catch you off guard. If you and I are not careful, the mention of her name, let alone her presence, can knock you off your feet and take the wind out of your sails. Any confidence you have can be shut down after she enters the room or opens her mouth. She just seems to have it all together, more highly favored, the one to envy.

But for whatever ways she is gifted or beautiful or admirable, there will never be a woman like you. Never. If you study science, you will see that your DNA can never be replicated, and your fingerprints are undeniably unique; your worth is set in stone from the very beginning.

A close friend put it so well: "I gave up friendships, leadership opportunities, and thousands of dollars in plastic surgeries. I settled for just okay in my walk with God, all because I got distracted long enough to take my eyes off the race, my race. The second you start getting curious about another girl's race, you wonder how she does it so well and why you don't, how she looks that good and why you don't measure up. These are not just thoughts; they are footholds, and they will lead to your downfall."

Human comparison ultimately blocks us from seeing the very beauty and strength of God in us. This hardwired identity of who we are will never be out of touch or out of strength or threatened by anything in this world. The Bible makes it really simple: "Do not conform any longer to the patterns of this world, but be transformed by the renewing of your minds. Then you will be able to test and approve what God's will is—his good, pleasing and perfect will" (Romans 12:2 NIV). Think about it; if we are so focused on building ourselves to be more of what the world esteems and perhaps better than her, we will keep our eyes off the invitation to want more. To want more is to want God. Deep down, we all crave for more than what we can see, articulate, or experience. This craving was put in us by God, to be fulfilled only by Him.

Here's a scenario of how our thoughts can go downhill fast: She pulled in the driveway after picking up her kids. There were leftover fast food bags and half-empty cups in the door holders, along with a few old fries and wrappers: typical mom van. It was going to be a great evening, she thought. She got the kids fed, and they did their homework. She was ready to unwind her tired mind. She sat down on the couch in her comfy clothes and began scrolling through social media feeds. At first, she enjoyed the funny posts and comments, but then it began to shift. More and more, she saw comments from other working moms and compared herself to them. They had worked out, took their children to the park, and done so much more. Suddenly, the guilt set in, and the comparison whispers spoke up: *How can she have all that extra time? How can she fit all of this in? How is she still so pretty and carefree? What is wrong with me? What am I doing wrong?*

Jennie Allen writes in her book *Restless*, "Nothing kills passions more than the fear of man, whether a quest for approval or nagging comparison. If we are running our race and our eyes are darting back and forth, we will not see the need around us. Hebrews 12:2 is stern about this. You want to run this race? You fix your eyes on Jesus."

The bottom-line truth to the above scenario is, don't worry about what anyone else is doing. We each have a glorious, messy, and uncharted race to run that holds power and holy purpose for all the world to see. As we all know, this requires more than just focus, more than just willpower, more than just a healthy friend group or good luck.

In her book *The Allure of Hope,* Jan Meyers says, "There is nothing new. Women have been trying to re-create themselves throughout history. A competition with other women, in the company of other women. It's a sport that goes far beyond tuning up physically or coming up with a new persona. We want to win. We want to ascend to goddesslike beauty without being reconciled with the Creator who breathed beauty into us."

Something along the way has caused us to doubt the safety of women and feel the need to compete, things like gossip, betrayal, offense, and envy. It speaks of a fallen and broken system, where you and I are prey to the stealthy work of a great and dangerous weapon called sin. Our pride tells us that we are the object of beauty, confidence, influence, and acceptance. We've all tasted rejection and suffering. It's part of this life, and it's painful and unpredictable. We can put up walls and try out new things, but fundamentally, we need to know there is a seat saved for us; in fact, it was created just for us by a gracious and loving God.

One thing that doesn't get talked about much, especially not publicly, is the secret comparisons mothers and daughters use to define themselves. I am not a mom of daughters but am close with many, and I know some of the internal struggles they face. There are so many delicate pressures within the influence on one another. Both mom and daughter hold a beauty and a humanity as they navigate their lives and their roles. Moms of girls, you are beautiful. You are enough. And it's not because of someone you raise or how she turns out, but because your beauty and worth have been determined by God. He calls you chosen. Please do not compare yourself to your daughter or put expectations on her that stem from unsettled areas in your own identity. It can be tempting, and sometimes we don't realize what we are doing. Your daughter is not an extension of you when it comes to reflecting your beauty. She doesn't determine your beauty or take away from it; you choose that and who you behold.

Daughters, your beauty and worth are not based on your mom. You have the freedom to decide where your source of beauty comes from. Do not feel obligated to imitate or avoid everything your mom does. God holds your worth and knows your deepest places. At each and every stage, He wants to write your unique story with you. Beauty flows from here.

I'm more convinced than ever that the enemy lurking around knows what happens when women empower women and work together for a common purpose: to build others up and spread the beauty from within them. This is a force to be reckoned with, a dangerous force for good that glorifies God and turns away from self-promotion and onto the greater mission. We were made to be a tribe on the same team, together, all wearing the same uniform. This is the greater work. So arise and take the risk; you have an irreplaceable seat at the table.

THE GLORIOUS TWIST

In actuality, comparison can be something great. All along, we were made to compare ourselves. We were not, however, made to compare ourselves against others. Robert Murray M'Cheyne sums it up this way: "For every [one] look at yourself, take ten looks at Christ. He is altogether lovely." Only godly comparison will lead us to humility, where we see our true selves in relation to Him and want more of Him and less of us. It is this kind of comparison where we learn that He offers us more than we could ever imagine or find on our own. "Therefore if anyone is in Christ, they are a new creation. The old is gone, the new has come" (2 Corinthians 5:17 NIV). Contrary to human comparison, which remains all about us, we will lose the temptation to look around at one another and keep score. We will instead crave what is brand new. We become more like Christ as we compare ourselves to Him, and our souls are gloriously filled.

Do not let the fear of what you are supposed to be drive you away from the beauty allotted just for you. The most special part about you is not how you fit in but how you stand out in a world who has never seen

> **The most special part about you is not how you fit in but how you stand out in a world who has never seen your kind of beauty.**

your kind of beauty. You are needed just as you are. You are rare, you are more precious than all the riches in the world, and you have been rescued by a valiant King. His name is Jesus, and He came to set you free, free from shame, addiction, and fear. His love for you is fierce and overwhelmingly good. It's more than your words could ever speak and better than your best-case scenario of who you want to be or look like. It will never fade or fail. It is what your heart longs for. He has so much more in store for you that only He can give you.

CONFIDENCE

Dictionary.com defines *confidence* as "belief in oneself and one's powers or abilities." Feeling sure of yourself and your abilities—not in an arrogant way, but in a realistic, secure way. Confidence isn't about feeling superior to others. According to Merriam-Webster, it's a quiet inner knowledge that you're capable.

We all crave confidence.

It is a quality that draws attention to every one of us. When it is used to build good in us and benefit others, it is an unstoppable force. The world has tried to bottle up the rights to confidence into some kind of magic formula. For us, we are wired to care about how we look. Whatever your body type, skin color, or size, God's design for you was diverse, often unassuming, compared to the rest of our culture. It's not based on your leadership abilities, the size of your social media platform, your body fat percentage, or your relationship status. Those things can describe you or fill out your bio, but they are temporary. There is nothing within ourselves that can provide the lasting confidence we need to fill us for this life. Unfortunately, we can hide behind just about anything for a little while and look like we've got it together.

For example, walking into a room full of other women can be competitive and nerve racking. The thoughts start slithering in: *She always looks gorgeous, she's engaged, she's always happy, she has the best family, she's pregnant, her house is perfect, she's so content, she has so many friends, her husband takes good care of her, and she always seems to get all the blessings, and I don't.* It's a breeding ground for the whispers that shout to all the areas of insecurity and tension and longings that swirl around us, armed and ready to attack.

Sadly, we have been programmed to cover up and hide the real us. Often, we are too busy trying to find more confidence instead of living with the confidence that we are enough. The influences around us celebrate illusions and appearances of confidence rather than the character itself. This happens in our workplace, playgroups, online dating, social media posts, women's ministry, and a variety of other places. Always show your best side; don't apologize or let others see the real you. And when you've done that, strive to be better than those around you, and keep it up no matter what is happening in your private world.

But the reality is, we remain with a gaping hole inside that asks, who really sees me? When you can't stop thinking about how far you are from being enough, God whispers, "Look at Me, not yourself or those around you. I am your advocate and your rescuer; out of Me springs forth all you need. Let go of you, and lean into Me. Let Me be your source of confidence."

Whether you have lived your life with confidence can be answered pretty quickly, when it's all said and done. I recently got curious about what people on their deathbed had to say about life. Maybe it is because of my fear of regret and all I have seen working as a nurse or being in ministry or just being exposed to life-and-death situations in our world. Life seems to become much clearer when the end is near. I believe it is some of the most valuable, uninhibited wisdom that we can take in and learn from. These responses cross over time, space, midlife crises, and bucket lists. Bronnie Ware, a hospice nurse who wrote a book about the time she spent with dying patients, found that this was one of their biggest regrets: "I spent my life trying to be someone else. I wish I had had the courage to live a life true to myself, not the life others expected of me."

Isn't this true for us now? We always have to make the choice of how we will live. No matter where we are in life, or how big or small it seems, we have a story to live out. And that very story is about a destiny of you being fully you and not someone else. Only God knows the end, and He is molding and shaping you as we speak.

The secret to real and true confidence does not come from you or me. We are, in fact, all recipients of a greater confidence that can never be taken away. Next to His power and majesty, every other method will fade away. Our greatest efforts are no match to His. After all, we were never meant to compete. He is our strong tower. He is our hiding place. He is our rock that we stand on. All other sources are false idols of security and will not last. The challenge for most of us is, we must first let go of the very places we hold so dear.

"You give me your shield of victory, and your right hand sustains me; you stoop down to make me great" (Psalm18:35 NIV).

> **You are more than what you're known for in this world. More than your resume.**

You are more than what you're known for in this world. More than your resume. More than your beauty or skill or talent. More than your finances, and the list goes on. The unmet desires in your heart, and the labels that continue to haunt you, have no hold on you. It's that thing that holds a grip deep down that you can't imagine will ever go away; you may have given up asking.

Those are the very places that the roots need to be ripped out so they can no longer choke us. The reason I know this is not based on a goal sheet or an interview. It's based on big and bold truths we can live in this life that provide more confidence than we could ever need: "greater is He that is in you than he that is in the world" (1 John 4:4 NIV). Each and every day, there is a harvest of good things waiting. We have been made alive with breath in our lungs because we belong to a higher power source, Who holds victory. God has a greater plan to rescue and restore whatever has tried to destroy you. It is the redemptive, good news of the Gospel.

Corrie ten Boom, a Christian hero known for hiding Jews from the Nazis during the Holocaust, said, "It is not my ability, but my response to God's ability, that counts."

You don't have to try harder. You were made to be emptied and then filled with the very purpose and strength that can move mountains. It's not because of a certain season, relationship status, or dress size that you possess this belief. You have always had it because you and I are a product of divine design. Confidence lies here.

> To the ones who used to be skinny or feel attractive,
> To the one who feels like she has nothing to offer,
> To the one who is still waiting for a soulmate,
> To the one deemed infertile, who longs for motherhood,
> To the one who has faced adultery,
> To the one who can't expose her secret,
> To the one who used to be healthy and now faces illness,
> To the one who was adopted or grew up in foster care,
> To the one who had an abortion,
> To those who had to grow up too fast and couldn't be kids,
> To the one using her body for money,
> To the one who can't see anything good in the mirror and starves herself, binges and gorges, or thinks that cutting will release some of the pain,
> To the one who is valued for her appearance and yet continuously feels empty,
> To those plagued with mental health struggles or addictions, who long to feel alive and free,
> To the stay-at-home mom who feels anonymous and just wants to find a piece of her again.

Despite whatever lingering season or circumstance, you represent a piece of God's glory that will never fade or disappear, no matter what the outer layers display. So let us run to Him and hold on tight. He's not finished yet.

"Being confident of this, that He who began a good work in you will carry it on to completion until the day of Christ Jesus" (Philippians 1:6 NIV).

COMPROMISE

This means accepting less of one thing in return for more of another (CTpost/living/Julia Bekker).

Fashion meets modesty.

Modesty comes from the Latin word *modestus,* which means "keeping within measure" (vocabulary.com).

In our world, modesty is not a popular concept. Perhaps it has gotten misunderstood as boring or out of touch with today's culture. To intentionally choose not to show off all the assets you were given as a woman may seem like such a waste. After all, aren't we supposed to show off what we have? It has become the norm for women and girls to expose more and more of themselves to draw attention. If we're honest, what used to be called scandalous and dishonorable is now very much in style. What used to be sacred and valuable is now on display for the world to see.

It was another hot sunny day at the water park, with lots of activity as crowds gathered to beat the summer heat. Buses dropped off loads of kids with their counselors feverishly doing headcounts. Lines formed outside, some for tickets and others for swim bag checks and season passes. Moms rushed to find shaded umbrella seats to keep their little ones covered from the hot sun, and teens were dropped off for the day. The party music pumped loudly over the speakers, and the smell of the grill starting up in preparation for the lunch crowd filled the water park.

That's when I saw her. She appeared to be in her late teens, wearing a skimpy thong bikini that accentuated every curve and drew every eye. My heart was broken for her as I watched her play in the waves, barely covered for all to see. She was in a small group of girls and guys who enjoyed the water park's rides and amenities. She appeared unfazed by it all, while many turned their heads to stare at her body with lingering, lustful looks.

As my kids and I left the park and were waiting for the tram to pick us up, I saw her again. As she walked by, she had a small T-shirt over her swimsuit and her bag slung over her shoulder. You wouldn't have thought much of it, until you saw her from behind, her backside still completely exposed for whoever wanted to see. Maybe no one ever told her the treasure she is, or maybe she didn't believe it. Maybe she doesn't know that she holds a royal beauty inside of her. She, like you and I, are daughters of the highest King more valuable than any fashion trend. Our bodies really are a rare and precious gift, worth keeping covered. They are, in fact, sacred. Although perhaps subtle, the war for her was in full effect that day at the water park.

THE GIFT OF MODESTY

These days, it's hard to keep anything private; just look at the social media feeds on your cell phone. There is so much pressure to use whatever you have to promote your beauty and somehow dictate your worth. God has given us a gift, and we hold a treasure. We as women were made beautiful and designed to display our beauty to bless the world and show the splendor of God from the inside out. We also need protecting from taking this gift to be a measuring stick it was never supposed to be. In 2 Corinthians 4:7 (NIV), we are given a powerful analogy of ourselves as "treasures in jars of clay to show that this all-surpassing power is from God and not from us." It reminds us of two critical points: a glimpse of who we are in comparison to our Creator, and a value within us that cannot be matched by anything this world has to offer.

Don't throw in the towel of your royal position. Too often, we women don't live out the promises God has spoken over our lives. We can say yes and amen, only to turn back and let our minds and bodies be sabotaged by the messages of this world. Our minds want to remind us of all the times we failed, we were hurt, or we were taken advantage of. Jesus came to earth and died so we could be set free from the slavery of our minds and our tendencies that can so quickly drift.

This war has been going on longer than any of us could ever know. It begins as harmless poses, trying to look cute in the mirror, that turn into posts with followers who give us more attention than we thought. We never meant for it to go further, but it does, and moral lines get crossed. Because if we stay where we are, the longing to feel beautiful and be noticed grows bigger. We can easily find ourselves chasing something or someone to feel beautiful, often lurking with consequences of our morality and our reputation. It seems to be louder in the dark and secret places. Isn't that where evil and sin do their best work? It's where our God-given needs of being seen and valued collide with the world and the tempting answers it offers us to linger there.

The beautiful young woman at the water park was not a prize to be bought but a God-made creation to be revered; the same goes for all females. The war is on for our beauty, our value, our bodies, and our identity, and it's not going away. We will have to make a choice of who or what we follow, or others will try to make the choice for us.

The question is, where are you looking to find your worth? You can take all the selfies and use all the filters to look flawless. You can get all the enhancements and spend all your money to meet a beauty standard, but still come up short. You can hand out autographs and have articles written about you and people wanting to follow you, but it will never satisfy. You can get the engagement ring, the house, the car, and the promotion, but your worth will never be found there. You can wish you were someone else and spend all your efforts trying to be her. For most of us, we've been searching but have been stuck looking in the wrong places. Don't get me wrong; it is a great thing to want to look your best, enjoy fashion and take good care of yourself. It was just never meant to be where your value and worth come from. The Bible speaks of an invitation: "Come all you who are thirsty. Give ear and come to me; hear me, that your soul may live. I will make an everlasting covenant with you" (Isaiah 55:1a, 3 NIV).

We are thought about, we are seen, and we are noticed long before we realize. We are not a project to be worked on, but rather a product of perfect and lasting love.

We are thought about, we are seen, and we are noticed long before we realize. We are not a project to be worked on, but rather a product of perfect and lasting love.

CONTROL

SECRETS

A secret is "something that is kept or meant to be kept unknown or unseen by others" (Oxford Dictionary).

Secrets have the power to cripple even the strongest of women.

When our inside life doesn't match the outside, we are forced to work harder to perform for ourselves and others. The chase to feel and look complete when life remains messy happens to all of us. And it all comes with a price. The aim for perfection and beauty and conflict-free relationships requires us to find a place to hide the aches, the longings, and the pain. Not only is this exhausting, but it can quickly lead us to burnout, depression, anxiety, and even self-harm. We become an open target for attacks that can open more doors for secrets and scars with our name attached. It can be such a vicious cycle.

Several years ago, in a Bible study at my church, I learned a whole other side about secrets. This new understanding changed my relationship with God forever. Beth Moore, a beloved and powerful Bible teacher, spoke a glorious revelation about this very word. The study was called *Sacred Secrets*. In it, she walked us through the negative, traditional view of the word *secret* that we are all familiar with and the power it holds to destroy, but she uncovered another view. She broke down the word in a whole different perspective that spoke about this intimate and amazing hidden life we get to have between us and God. She included scripture and challenged us with a new view of this secret life: What if all along, this space was meant to be between you and your Savior in a place like your closet or your most sacred, secret place? What if this is really how good God is, to want our deepest, darkest, most painful, and shame-ridden secrets so He can carry them and lead us to that place of actual freedom? This allows Him to begin to teach us "wisdom in the secret place" (Psalm 51:6 NIV).

I learned about true and lasting intimacy with God, rather than withholding from Him the deepest battles of my private life. Breaking through food's grip on me began as an invitation in the dark, where I hid. It proceeded to become a battle that I was invited to face in secret, messy places no one else knew even existed. It was there in the battle with trembling, weakness, and shame that I experienced the very power of God in me. It was a brand-new strength coming forth out of the exact place I had failed the most. This was not my battle to fight all along, but I had tried for so long. I began to see Him as more than Lord or Savior, but as my most intimate friend and soulmate; that left me speechless. He, our high priest and friend, is the

One Who sympathizes with every one of our weaknesses, temptations, and secrets. He is right there with us (see Hebrews 4:15).

Isaiah 45:3 (NIV) declares, "I will give you treasures in the darkness, riches stored in secret places, so that you may know that I am the Lord, the God of Israel, who summons you by name."

An amazing secret came out of this new season. It was an internal shift that had been happening before I acted on it. I often didn't realize I was being changed and made aware of self-control. Something in me, the Holy Spirit, was strengthening me. It was no longer my willpower trying to withstand temptation. In *Sacred Secrets,* Moore writes, "You and I get to decide what's going to be the secret. We're going to come out before God with that which is dangerous, poisonous, toxic and dark. We're going to come into the light. We will never be lighter or freer than when our secrets land somewhere safe." None of the stories and situations we have encountered are too much for Him.

So whether we're outwardly showing evidence of war or inwardly gasping for air, our value remains. "God is able to redeem *every* situation. He is able to breathe new life into *every* heart. God is able to restore anything that's been lost or broken or stolen. He is able to do far more than we dare ask or imagine" (Ephesians 3:21 CEV).

ANXIETY

The Oxford Dictionary defines *anxiety* as "a feeling of worry, nervousness, or unease, typically about an imminent event or something with an uncertain outcome."

Ever since I was a young girl, I have had battles with fear and felt the sting of anxiety. When my voice and my strength were buried beneath the shouts in my head, it quickly became an unwelcome guest in my mind as I watched it play out in life situations that I felt trapped in. In those times, all the rational thoughts and reassuring self-coaching I could offer myself were silenced by the grip of fear.

The stress in our minds can send us in a tailspin of scenarios and physical symptoms that we don't see coming. It's like an invisible wave washing over you that you can't prepare for, and it knocks you straight down. It's not a splash. It's a complete submersion that disorients you; you can't find which way is up, and you just can't catch a breath. Sometimes, it's obvious, and other times, it's subtle. Our minds can overtake us when we least expect it and suck the strength and peace right out of us.

Not too long ago, I took a trip with some friends for a fortieth birthday celebration. It started out with a cute selfie in the airport on the way to Costa Rica, of all places. It was a new experience to travel that far by myself. I rehearsed a pep talk in my head for several weeks: "You're a mature adult, a strong mom with a college degree and a house. People do this all the time. You can do this by yourself." But the flood of icy panic in my chest was not eased by this speech. The fear would rise, and the thoughts followed as I waited at the gate to board and then sat in my airplane seat: *Where is my passport? Is the airplane safe? What if I get sick? What if I lose my purse, my phone, my luggage? Will something horrible happen to one of my kids or my husband while I'm gone?* It was a plague of worst-case scenarios that can take over and bombard me under even the most pleasant of situations. Why does panic overtake me like a sudden rushing wave? Why can't I just control it?

It is a funny thing to be leading others and encouraging them and lifting them out of their despair when the anxiety hits you, and the echoes of panic strike. None of us are immune to fear. For me, the hard-hitters come when I feel all alone in a familiar group or in the middle of the night, when I feel consumed by darkness. It's the invisible war at hand, and it's not going away. So many of us deal with mental health challenges, and it's affecting more and more every day. We know more than ever that our world is longing for safety and peace from all the unrest and chaos happening. In her book *Uninvited,* Lysa TerKeurst writes that we need to keep watch over our minds. She says, "You don't have to go to Africa to get stalked by a lion. There's a roaring lion waiting just around every next thought you think. He's a defeated foe who has already suffered a fatal blow. But before he falls, he'll try to make a few last kills. With everything he's got left, he's coming after your mind" (see 1 Peter 5:8).

Our minds shout for a Savior to rescue us. What if we came, with unfiltered desperation, to the God who created the very mind we think with, the same one we love and hate with? The Bible talks quite a lot about this war over our minds and the thoughts that come through. Second Corinthians 10:5 (NIV) says, "We demolish arguments and every pretension that sets itself up against the knowledge of God, and we take every thought captive and make it obedient with Christ." What Paul is saying is not every thought that we think is worthy of us believing or allowing. In fact, most of them are flaming arrows, looking to harm us. The answer is not more self-esteem, self-help, goal-markers, self-meditation, or self-anything. The answer, through Jesus, comes with a force of calming power and supernatural peace that no one can fully explain or match.

For so many years, without realizing it, I accepted food as my friend, and it took every opportunity to take over my life. My heart was starving in other areas, and the enemy offered to fill me with an alternative that felt comforting. My appetite to feel full had not changed, but my standards sure did. I needed a companion I could count on, and I grew desperate. I wanted something to fill me, to distract me, to excite me when I was lonely, scared, or bored.

As the habit grew and the pleasure of indulgence hit deep down in me, it became something I couldn't turn off. I was flooded with shame and vowed never to do it again. I would exercise frequently and obsess over my body image, disgusted by what I saw in the mirror. I was desperate for a way out. I often contemplated purging but never could bring myself to go through with it. Looking back, it was God's grace over me that didn't allow this to happen because I probably wouldn't have stopped. All along, He was wooing me to offer me more, but I didn't know it. He had better plans for me, but I couldn't see anything through the lens of shame and disappointment, except a body that was too far gone. I needed new eyes to see.

"When you pass through the waters, I will be with you; and when you pass through the rivers, they will not sweep over you. When you walk through the fire, you will not be burned; the flames will not set you ablaze" (Isaiah 43:2 NIV).

No longer do I walk alone. Even though stress, anxiety, and fear still happen, I am one prayer away from connecting safely back with Him again. He longs to be with me. How can that be true? I've messed up, I've sinned, I've worshipped false idols, I've doubted so much, and I've chosen to go my own way without Him, so many times.

It's His consuming love that woos me back and speaks to me. Anything less than a divine intervention would not be enough. Just because you fall down doesn't mean you have to stay there. God is our "very present help in trouble" (Psalm 46:1 ESV). He is there with us. We get to anticipate and be ready to receive from Him as we are met by the forces of good fighting on our behalf.

Sandra L. Coates

HIDING OUT IN PLAIN SIGHT

Macmillan Dictionary defines *hiding* as "to go or be somewhere where no one can find you or see you."

Genesis 3:6 (NIV) says, "When the woman saw that the fruit of the tree was good for food and pleasing to the eye, and also desirable for gaining wisdom, she took some and ate it." All the way back to the book of Genesis, we see the desire to hide as a result of our actions. Adam and Eve had been told by God that life would be never be the same if they chose to go past the boundaries He set before them. Eve listened to the outside influences and misinterpretations of the truth, and then she passed it on. She used her own senses to make the decision to eat from the specific tree God had said not to. When they realized they were naked, they hid. It's a funny thing we learn regarding what shame does to us when we mess up. We find ourselves having no choice but to want to take cover. Ultimately, this leads us away from the forgiveness and mercy of God that we so desperately want.

Psychologists will tell you that one of the greatest fears of women is the fear of being alone (Karin Arndt, *Psychology Today*). Somehow, we can go everywhere else besides God for help when we feel alone and isolated. We all prefer to avoid pain. It can feel out of control and never

The real problem is not our struggle, but rather the appearance that nothing is wrong. On the outside, we can appear fine, while one layer deeper, we are tragically not.

ending. The real problem is not our struggle, but rather the appearance that nothing is wrong. On the outside, we can appear fine, while one layer deeper, we are tragically not. We see this all too often in Hollywood, in our communities, in our churches, and in our own homes. The greater question is not if we have pain, but where do we go with our pain and the desire to be free from it?

It can feel so much better to hide, hide from our appearance, our past, our insecurity. Often, it can feel safer to hide behind our successes so no one sees the real us. We all long to feel safe, out in the open, confident and secure in ourselves. That desire is in all of us, no matter what age or season we are in. Something always seems to be trying to disqualify us, trying to make us compare ourselves to others, or consuming us with all the things we're not good at. It's an age-old tactic that still messes with us today. Whether we know it or not, there is a race marked out for us that was intentionally set before we were born. It contains both challenging and glorious elements that guide us through uncharted territory.

Hiding can just feel safer. It happens when I feel like I can't do anything well, when the social media feed confirms my insecurities of not being enough, or when my house, my body, or my relationships don't meet my expectations. I lose sight of the very seal of God's promise over my life and every breath He gives me. But God tells us, in our weaknesses, He is strong. That is how our God works. "He uses the weak things of the world to shame the strong. He chose the lowly things of this world and the despised things—and the things that are not—to nullify the things that are, so no one can boast" (2 Corinthians 1:28 NIV). In my weakness, I turn to the tower who is my helper and my strength.

Sometimes, our circumstances feel like a prison cell, and if we're honest, it can feel safer to stay back and fight our battles alone, under our control. It's risky to desire more, to reach out and find community and friendships, where people remember you and pursue more than just the obligatory pleasantries. The glaring questions resound: "What if there is nothing more? What if God doesn't come through? What if I never fit in?" Instead, we get to ask, "What if I was already fully chosen as a daughter of the

King? What if I already did fit in?" By exposing our questions and seeking answers, we are brought closer to the path of acceptance and heavenly hope.

It is no surprise that suicide and mental health issues plague us today. We all experience extreme pain and trials on this side of heaven. Some of us experienced detestable trauma and darkness that make it hard to cope. As a nation, people are suffering from mental illness in unprecedented numbers, including young girls who feel the pressures all too soon. Both women and girls are greatly impacted, and some are dying over the pressures they face. Others feel like they need to hide behind impossible standards. There is a desperation for peace in our souls that the world cannot satisfy. Apart from Jesus, we are all searching to find a place where we don't need to do any more, be something better, or look prettier, to no longer be outcasts or achieve more or prove something. It seems we all really want the same things: acceptance, happiness, feeling chosen, hitting the marks that make us feel successful and beautiful. God knows how deep these needs are within us too, and He wants to meet us there.

NO LONGER DISQUALIFIED

In John 4:1–26, a woman of no position, no noble status, and no future ahead of her encountered Jesus. To be found out regarding her sins and many failed marriages would uncover her shame for all to see. She decided the safest time to draw water from the well would be in the heat of the day, when no one else was there to see her. She had no idea that she would encounter the safest, most powerful, and inviting human ever to walk this earth. He was not bound by culture or ritual, but He was on a special assignment to see her. He would take notice of her, not as an object but as a woman with purpose.

She was a Samaritan, and in that culture, she was not in the same category as the Jews. She was not to even use their dishes, let alone be seen speaking to Him. He revealed the truth about herself that she never spoke out loud and offered her a life she could never imagine qualifying for. She had failed too often and had too many reminders of her consequences. But that day was different because He saw her for something more than a woman who was sinful; He offered her a new life and she accepted it. Jesus said, "Whoever drinks the water I give them will never thirst again" (John 4:14a NIV). We must go to the One Who sees us for more and offers us a new name, a new start, no matter our past. He changed her life forever that day, and she would go on to share her divine encounter with the world.

It's no coincidence that our biggest battles involve us being alone: separated or in competition with other women. Ironically, hiding and isolation make us actually more vulnerable to attacks. We weren't meant to stay hidden. Together, we have power to help one another; together, we can fight for one another and share the load. And when we can't bear the pressure, we stand together to say, "I know what you mean because I've been there too. See my scars? Girl, you're not alone."

God wants all of our secrets, our mess-ups, our hidden places. We don't have to worry; they are safe with Him. He is the faithful One we can trust.

PERFECTIONISM

Creating unrealistically high expectations for ourselves that become self-critical when we do not achieve those high expectations. Setting expectations that we can never meet and then criticizing ourselves because we don't meet them. In perfectionistic mode, we are constantly focusing on ways to improve, and there is little affirmation or encouraging self-talk. (Becky Van Valin)

THE MYTH OF SUPERWOMAN

(This title was taken from Edmond Bourne's *The Anxiety and Phobia Workbook*.)

We all know it, the impossible measuring stick we impose on ourselves to please, to perform, to create the perfect version of ourselves. I have followed this trend time and time again. When I fall into these traps of perfectionism, I lose myself. I become tossed around by my own slave-driving mentality, and I am never satisfied. If I'm not careful, my own thoughts can replace the truths that I believe about myself, and I spiral down. Joy and peace are nowhere in sight. It's such a struggle to extend grace to myself or think about all the good things in my life. The truth is, we will always come up short in our human attempts to achieve perfection. It's important to take a deep breath and realize that God doesn't want us to be perfect. He never asks us to take on this role, and He knows we can never achieve it.

"You don't have to be the perfect one. The perfect one has already come" (Priscilla Shirer).

You may think you need the perfect body, skin color, personality, family, or relationship with God. It can feel like so much pressure, and there may never be a word spoken about it. Why do we try to be all put together? Why do I expect perfection out of others? These standards will never be enough, either. Let's be thankful that we weren't designed to have it all together; we weren't designed to fit a mold. So whatever you're going through (feeling scattered, unproductive, frustrated, envious, overlooked, hopeless, fearful, or something else), take courage, and know you have complete access to the perfect One.

Perfectionism brings about frustration for the person trying to live up to it, but also for others who feel like they cannot meet that standard set by someone else. It's a lose-lose, wherever you fall in the process. There is little freedom from the perfectionism bondage until you step out of it, surrendering to Jesus and giving yourself permission to not meet the set standards. This is where we can experience a new road, where we put down homemade weapons and ammunition, and cover our vulnerable places with a new kind of armor. We are offered this lifestyle, not by our own pursuit or determination, but rather, by our own surrender.

To surrender is not a defeat; it is being able to see a greater force available to wage war for us against the enemy at hand. If we don't know it now, we will need to suit up for this battle because, yes, we will get dirty and probably endure some wounds. Putting on the full armor of God means walking the narrow road, one only a few will find (see Matthew 7:13–14). At many points, I have wanted to be among those few, but I was far too easily pleased by the world and defeated by what everyone else was saying around me. Those things had to die in order for me to see the truth and freedom that was waiting for me to receive and take hold of.

IT'S NEVER GOING TO BE PERFECT

On average, we have sixty thousand thoughts per day, with approximately 80 percent of those being negative (*Faith, Hope and Psychology*). No wonder God tells us to "take every thought captive to make it obedient to Christ" (2 Corinthians 10:5 NIV). We are overloaded with our thoughts. It's a war zone inside of our heads that can be a constant sabotage if we let it. Before we know it, the narrative in our head has started. It's an involuntary thing that happens, and we don't even know it's there until we're down a path we never signed up for.

Her house is so perfect, rolled through my mind as she invited me in. I was immediately aware of my unkempt house, stained shirt, and car filled with used toys and old goldfish crackers. She joyfully greeted me at the door while her sweet baby played behind her on the beautiful clean carpet, smiling as I came in. I admired her lovely smelling home and shiny kitchen while she poured me a cup of coffee, and then we sat down to catch up on each other's lives. I noticed the gorgeous wedding photo, the vacation pictures, and the chronological baby years captured in frames on the wall. Why did it seem so effortless to her? I couldn't help but notice every dish was perfectly placed, there was no evidence of stains or crumbs, every toy had its place, and the crockpot simmered away with a delicious dinner. She exuded what I longed to have: contentment in the season of motherhood while feeling alive in taking care of my home and raising my family. I was struck with inner interrogation and subtle attacks that usually started off with questions like, "What *was* I good at?"

"Why couldn't I be happy and content in what I had?"

"Why do I always need someone to help me out of my pit?"

"Why can't I just be joyful with the blessings of my kids in this season that everyone says goes so fast, so enjoy every minute?"

"Why did continuing to work make me feel like a better mom, even though it would be so much better to fully commit to one or the other and not feel like you're doing the minimum at everything?"

We all matter more than we know. We matter because God deems us worthy, and not for any other reason out there. Whether it is someone we raise, teach, or encourage, we all have great things to contribute that

> **We all matter more than we know. We matter because God deems us worthy, and not for any other reason out there.**

have kingdom impact. We must first look past ourselves, past the stained shirt and crumbs on the floor and all the expectations we thought we could meet to really see that God has so much more for us that will exceed what we could imagine. Galatians 6:9 (NIV) says, "So let us not become weary in doing good, for at a proper time we will reap a harvest if we do not give up."

Heaven awaits us, but we are not there yet. We are on a mission, like an athlete training for the Olympics, with our eye on the gold medal. Do we know our God has given us all the weapons we need to fight? We are stronger than we think because of Him, but we need to remember this is not our fight to win. To be sold out for Christ means our focus cannot be on ourselves but rather on the One Whose armor we wear. It's not about all our prayers being answered, or a wrong being made right, or our failures. It's simply not about us. It's all about Jesus increasing in and through us as we continue to decrease in focus. "Forgetting what is behind and straining toward what is ahead, I press on toward the goal to win the prize for which God has called me heavenward in Christ Jesus" (Philippians 3:13–14 NIV).

Reflection/Discussion

What about the War Inside?

Reflection: Where do you see the war happening in our world? What about our generations of women? What about in you?

Exercise: What has tried to take you down or disqualify you?
Review the four Cs:

- comparison
- confidence
- compromise
- control

Truth: We are all encounter battles. Whatever battles you are facing right now are not being fought alone. "Sovereign Lord, my strong deliverer, you shield my head in the day of battle" (Psalm 140:7 NIV).

Big Idea: The greatest war ever battled has already been won by God Himself over sin, destruction, and death. As we claim Jesus as our risen King, we stand in the victory He completed as we face the messes and trials in our lives.

Now go back and write a new war tactic over each battle you have encountered as you stand firm and claim God's victory over your life.

PART 3

Examining Beauty

This commercial tagline is an oldie but a goodie: "Maybe she's born with it. Maybe it's Maybelline." Women of every age, race, and culture have been wired to be image-bearers of beauty. We didn't come up with the idea of what it was all supposed to look like or all the ways it would be expressed, but it's undeniably part of our culture. Industries have labored to find just the right formula for us with their miraculous products and glowing promises of glamour. It's what the internet, social media platforms, Pinterest, and fashion designers around the world have tried to bring to life. There are endless faces in our world that bear hours of work, money, and time spent trying to perfect beauty. In 2020, the beauty industry was worth approximately $97 billion. The cosmetic surgery industry makes more than $16 billion annually, with the United States having the largest cosmetic industry in the world (Statista/dealsonhealth.net).

As a culture, we are preoccupied with ourselves and our outside appearances. There is no question that we care about how we look; we want to invest in staying healthy and looking our best. The issue becomes how far we go to achieve this goal, if there is such a thing as the perfect face, skin color, body type, or look. We give more money and attention to achieving the most beautiful version of ourselves. If we can't get it naturally, we've invented clever ways to make ourselves appear beautiful and flawless. Photoshop technology and other editing programs let us airbrush and alter body parts to match the latest and greatest looks. Somehow, it doesn't need to be real, just convince onlookers it is real. The result is driving women and girls into a false beauty pit that is completely unattainable or cosmetic enhancements that offer them temporary solutions. All the while, the desperate search to feel secure and beautiful continues.

LOOKING BACK ON BEAUTY

Growing up, I was a big doll fan and held those plastic beauties in my hands for hours at a time, but I think Barbie may have tainted many young minds. It pains me to say that, being such a fan of hers, but it's just too important not to explore how our minds have been shaped. Who thought it was a good idea to make perfect dolls as role models for young girls? It may seem like a harmless pastime, but compared to the chubby dolls we played with, she was much different. Did she become a Miss America model overnight, or did she just stop eating when she hit puberty? Did she start the grinding workouts when she realized being pretty required much more?

I may be overexaggerating just a bit, but you get the point. An article on Rehabs.com said this about her: "Although she's long been considered the universal *ideal* for a woman's figure, an analysis of her doll-size shape in proportion to a fully grown woman shows Barbie is anatomically impossible and would be reduced to walking on all fours and incapable of lifting anything. The shocking experiment by Rehabs.com is aimed at those with eating disorders who are sadly 'dying to be Barbie.'"

Barbie quickly became quite an influence, a standard, if you will, of what the ideal woman should look like. No one really knew the impact this tiny plastic woman would have on the billions of girls who studied her frame and matched her clothes and brushed her hair for hours on end. But it subtly became ingrained over the younger years of their lives. Her clothes, her lifestyle, her dream house were all just so attractive and inviting for all seasons. She took your mind off of reality with hours of imagination and play. No one really stopped to think her body was drastically disproportionate; to look that way, she could've been anorexic, probably in and out of the hospital, hair falling out, and no muscle tone. She definitely would not be able to prance around town with Ken in the Barbie car and high heels. It was as if a match was lit on a line of gasoline that spread like wildfire to a world wanting a mold, and she was the one to watch.

Interestingly, if we go back much further in time, when curves were the thing, you get quite a different model of beauty. Back in the late 1800s, if you didn't have curves and extra weight on you, you weren't getting your portrait taken because you were not among the beautiful or the privileged. In her article "Did Our Ancestors Go on Weight Loss Diets?" Ellen Van Houten writes, "For a woman to have extra weight on her body was a symbol of beauty, fertility and wealth." Women were considered important and attractive if they had excess fat, what we would consider obese. Back then, to be thin was considered poor, lacking in proper nutrition or health.

Or even more recently, find a picture of Norma Jean Baker (aka Marilyn Monroe), the sizzling Hollywood icon. She graced magazine covers in her curvy body that varied between size 8 and 12. She appeared carefree, joy-filled, and glowing in her most famous photos, while behind it all, she fought the humble beginnings in foster homes, suffered from mental illness throughout her life, and experienced several failed marriages and miscarriages. Her life on camera did not match her life off camera. Tragically, at the age of thirty-six, she took her own life, making the case that beauty in and of itself can mask so much darkness and pain inside.

Despite all of the famous poses and iconic photographs, in the end, it became too much for her to bear.

In her book, *Uninvited*, Lysa TerKeurst writes, "The spotlight never fixes our insecurities. It only magnifies what we thought popularity would cover up." Apart from a lasting and true source of beauty, the limelight is not strong enough to hold us up.

A longtime expert in the fashion industry is Carey Lewis, the founder of Actors, Models & Talent for Christ (AMTC), which is a world-recognized talent development ministry.

Here is what she writes in *Finding Beauty*:

> My mother was a New York fashion model in the late 1940s. My daughter is a New York fashion photographer, and I've spent my whole life in the beauty business. I know how to polish "diamonds in the rough," and I know how to make "plain" people look attractive. I've seen models turn anorexic and almost die. I've seen girls who never had a date in high school become cover girls. I've seen people with incredible potential go nowhere from a lack of confidence. I've seen popular girls enjoy the spotlight— too much. I also know what it's like to feel ugly. I was the fat daughter of a beautiful mother. I weighed 290 pounds when I was 16—and eventually peaked at 360 pounds on my 36th birthday. I know what it's like to be transformed, by losing 220 pounds and keeping them off for 25 years. This was through the grace of a God who helped me, even before I knew His Son.

Here's the thing about beauty: Everybody's got it. It's not fickle, because God's not fickle. It's not a certain size, look, weight, hairstyle or outfit. It's confidence found in Christ. It's the sparkle in your eyes. It's kindness in your smile. It's pep in your step. Yes, polish helps the shine, because beauty can be covered—but the glow is still there, waiting to brighten every place you go. In God's eyes, you're already a masterpiece. When you begin to see yourself the way God sees you, your own transformation will happen. Your outside will begin to reflect your inside.

Statistics say over 95 percent of women do not see themselves as beautiful. A staggering number of women today are lonely and depressed; they have a poor body image, eating disorders, and low self-esteem. We find ourselves feeling insecure and compare ourselves to some imagined version of how we're supposed to look and feel. The pressure to be perfect and accomplished and slim—all with a smile—is exhausting. It's not the way it is supposed to be. It robs us of the very thing we have possessed all along: true and lasting beauty, value, and purpose, regardless of what we see in the mirror.

If we look deeper, we were not the only ones who thought of beauty as something to take hold of. There was another one who shared this obsession of self and the alluring power brought by being the most beautiful. Here is his description; you may know him as Satan:

> This is what the Sovereign Lord says: "You were the model of perfection, full of wisdom and perfect in beauty. You were in Eden, the garden of God; every precious stone adorned you: ruby, topaz and emerald, chrysolite, onyx and jasper, sapphire, turquoise and beryl. Your settings and mounting were made of gold; on the day you were

created they were prepared. You were anointed as a guardian cherub, for so I ordained you. You were on the holy mount of God; you walked among the fiery stones. You were blameless in your ways from the day you were created til wickedness was found in you. Through your widespread trade you were filled with violence, and you sinned. So I drove you in disgrace from the mount of God, and I expelled you, O guardian cherub, from among the fiery stones. Your heart became proud on account of your beauty, and you corrupted your wisdom because of your splendor. So I threw you to the earth." (Ezekiel 28:12–17 NIV)

When I read this description, I am quickly awakened to the opposing sides of beauty and the war at hand. It's fierce and flashy, with a constant fight for first place. It is nothing new today. We've been tricked by culture and our world, where the enemy resides, to see beauty as a human-made marker of worth. The perfection of God Himself, Who crafted us

> **We've been tricked by culture and our world, where the enemy resides, to see beauty as a human-made marker of worth.**

and planted His beauty in us from our conception, was not enough. We needed to be more than everyone else. Therefore, the mentality now is, do whatever it takes to work harder, look prettier, be more fit, have better goals, and stay confident in your value as superior. You are the object of beauty and success; you are in control of your destiny. For some of us, that may not seem like a problem; perhaps it's an exaggeration. Let's face it; it can sound so good to keep striving to be the best. But for those who are weary of the pace, tired of the emptiness, and done with falling short, maybe it's time to stop and evaluate what beauty was intended to be.

❙ UNLOCKING THE TREASURE

Stasi Eldredge writes, "It breaks my heart when women look at the sky and think, 'Wow! God is amazing!' But look at the mirror and say 'Ugh!' As if he didn't not make both" (stasieldredge.com).

What if, all along, the world has tried to help us lose our understanding of the treasure we hold and our position of power? What if all the distractions and plans and promises for success never meant to answer the real questions? Today, we have more people than ever who are searching for their purpose, identity, or gender. We have more mental illness flooding our minds with fear and hopelessness. For all of us, there is a cry for help, for understanding, and for acceptance that we only know in part but is universal to us all. The attempts to use human rationality and popular belief to replace divine truth brings confusion and conflict. When we have the eyes to see the Master's plan, and turn away from the things of this world, we won't be so tempted to compromise for the counterfeit indulgences. Instead, "our hearts would swell with joy" (Isaiah 60:5 NIV), and we instead, will sit it in awe of the radiance and love available to us and in us.

Every woman recorded in Scripture who encountered God was shown a glimpse of the grandeur and distinct purpose of her life that she had never known. The majority of these women were looked down upon because of their lowly social status or their lifestyle choices (Samaritans and prostitutes, to name two). Because of His unrelenting love for these women, they (and all of us) witnessed what a true power source could do over perfection. Their previous track records and lack of influence were nowhere to be found when God Almighty stepped in. He would have the final say over their irreplaceable purpose, and their testimony would become a role model for us all.

It can be hard to find our place without fitting in. We are all on the lookout for where to safely land. It's where we can thrive and feel alive, yet still desire something greater to satisfy us for the long haul. We need more than what we see and experience. It may sustain us for a little while, but the source of joy or satisfaction just doesn't seem to last.

The enemy wants us to believe we planted the divisive, self-destructive thoughts in our head about ourselves or someone else. If he can keep us from experiencing God's mercy and get us to believe that we are what is wrong, or someone in our lives is the problem, then his job is done. We will take it from there and start the downward spiral of staying focused on the problem and all that we are not. We must know the radiant power we hold deep within us, that no one and no situation can touch.

If you never surrender your past, your pride, your shame, your addiction, or whatever has a label on you and tries to hold you down, you will remain in chains. Let me repeat that, a little louder (so to speak): You will remain bound to that thing that has false power over you. The only freedom is in releasing it to Jesus. Although it is probably aren't an outward confinement, the inward bondage is undeniable. In and of ourselves, there is no other remedy to free us from the pain, the emptiness, the sin of others and our own destructive selves. Only Jesus offers this freedom.

> **I had become my own greatest enemy and biggest stumbling block to the healing and freedom awaiting me.**

My greatest testimony is how God rescued me from myself. The biggest things in me that needed to die were the four Cs, which I addressed in the previous section: comparison, confidence, compromise, and control. I had become my own greatest enemy and biggest stumbling block to the healing and freedom awaiting me. All along, I was trying so hard to be someone better.

As a result of my rescue, God didn't stop with me; He chose to use my transformation to represent His beauty and His light and His confidence for all to see and experience for themselves. It wasn't mine to hold onto. I heard His voice loud and clear when He said to me, "I have an opportunity for you." It was at the end of a long season, where I felt stuck and had lost my zeal. I noticed anxiety and depression kept flaring up in me as I tried to keep pressing on, with a smile on my face. It was not enough and kept sucking the joy out of me. God knew I loved fashion and creative ways to connect with other women. He knew because He had placed those things in me. He knew I loved studying the art of confidence and seeing how confident women carried themselves, with a glow of wonderful purpose and humility. He knew my whole story and first wanted to show me a glimpse of what He was calling out in me. It is always more than we can think or imagine.

In *Unseen,* Sara Hagerty writes, "The wink of God: It comes when we believe He is capable of reaching tenderly and knowingly into our story. It comes when we believe He wants to intertwine His story with ours and tell our story back to us, His way."

SUNRISE, SURFING, AND AN ENCOUNTER WITH BEAUTY

It was a picture-perfect morning down at the beach. I arrived a few minutes before the sunrise, with my longboard in tow. The stillness of the morning was inviting, and I was excited to catch some waves that day. As I was waxing my board and doing some stretches, I began to see more people walking in the sand. Some of them still had sleep lines on their face and had just come from the hotels right behind them. Some were quietly talking as they found their spot to sit, and others had hoodies covering their heads, with no words at this hour of the morning. Some were comfortable sitting on beach towels, while others walked down by the water. They seemed to be enjoying the early morning beach scene, but I didn't realize they were also waiting for something.

All of a sudden, everything stopped as all eyes were on the horizon, out beyond the sea. There, the most beautiful sunrise peeked out over the water. I was in awe; we all were. The glorious light beamed across the entire beach as it rose higher and higher to announce the daylight. I smiled as I watched it all happen. God Himself was displaying a glimpse of His creation right in front of our eyes. His stunning beauty lit up everything around us, and people grabbed their phones or cameras to capture this moment. The light was beaming, and not one person there could take their eyes off the brilliant colors and majestic scenery.

At this time, it didn't matter who believed in God or knew anything about His Word, as all had been swept away by this magnificent wonder of nature. He was closer than anyone realized and more radiant than a photo or painting could capture. We watched for several minutes to see the first light turn into a beaming sun, emerging until the day had been declared and the light shone brightly on all our faces.

I strapped my leash around my ankle and grabbed my surfboard. As I waded into the ocean, hopped on my board, and started paddling, I began to wonder if that same grandeur of beauty that was before my eyes was also within me. *How could that be, God?* I thought. He was inviting me deeper to see. As I sat in the water, waiting for the next set of waves, with the sun now fully illuminating the day, my thoughts went deeper: *What if I already was beautiful? Was this beauty I had witnessed that morning really the same beauty He had put in me? But what I saw was so bright and so glorious; how could I ever compare? Maybe He really had been listening to my secret longings? I guess today He just wanted to show me.*

That morning, I encountered God's beauty through a sunrise, and something bigger shifted in me. I didn't realize it until later on, when the nasty whispers in my mind returned, and I caught myself tearing down who I was. A new mindset had surprisingly come to my rescue, and I began the journey of defending myself. It was a wonderful shift. I had been given fresh eyes to see and new weapons to fight with. With all that is in me, I believe the biggest battle capable of the greatest transformation happens when we realize who we have been all along, filled with an irreplaceable beauty and purpose that God wants to show us, over and over again. Is He just that good? The answer is yes. Yes, He is.

For all this time, the world has tried to nail down what beauty is. Outside of nature, the focus has largely been identified with sexuality, outward appearance, and popularity. God has always had a different view on beauty and worth than that. It's not based on what is popular or aesthetically pleasing. It originates from an inward and hidden place, where supernatural exchanges occur and marvelous goodness and light burst forth. Success, beauty, and confidence have never come from a platform we stand on, but rather an internal life transformed and walking in the victory set before us. We can stand in wonder at this, similarly to the close friends of Jesus who encountered this same wonder and said, "Who is this that even the winds and waves obey him?" (Mark 4:41 NIV).

We see this time and time again throughout the Gospels, where Jesus's interactions, His authority, and His submission send shockwaves through the world as He completed the mission He came to do. All we have to do is look at the life of Jesus and see what made Him beautiful. It was not His outward appearance or popularity. It was something far greater and lasting that drew every heart to want to know more of Him. He embodied beauty, complete with excruciating and glorious battle scars.

I may not know your secret battles, but I do know the One Who does. No one else may have seen these battles that you have fought or know the pain, scars, or hardness it's caused. But He has. He is strong, He is safe, and He is good. Best of all, He has a deep, unconditional love just for you that will take your breath away.

The cure begins with you discovering and believing who you *really* are:

- You were made all along to bear the image of One much greater than you.
- You were chosen to be unlike any other woman who has ever lived or ever will.
- You hold a permanent and unique beauty that is needed both for your destiny and to build others up.
- God breathed a purpose in you more valuable than any platform or influence this world has to offer.
- God's timing for your life is appointed, and you, His daughter, never needs to doubt His attention or take shortcuts when the journey gets daunting. You. Are. Enough.

When we can wrap our minds around these truths and accept them as ours, everything changes. It gets real and personal, and opportunity awaits far beyond our reach. We're not just another girl or another woman. God Almighty, the One everyone will one day bow down to in reverence, is actively working out your life and using every struggle and detour to do incredible things. He is more in love with you than anyone on this earth. When this fundamental truth is uncovered, with no strings attached, we will taste freedom like never before. It will become our anthem, our weapon to fight the opposition we face.

Reflection/Discussion

What about Your Beauty?

Reflection: What is beauty to you? What is considered beautiful to the world?

Exercise: Take some time to make a compare/contrast list.

Explain how your understanding of beauty has shaped your life.

What part of your life holds you down the most (appearance, age, background, relationship status, other)?

Truth: He made you with great care and purpose to be exactly the way you are.

"Those who look to the Lord are radiant; their faces are never covered with shame" (Psalm 34:5 NIV).

Big Idea: We all wrestle with not feeling beautiful or valuable enough. God wants you to experience His perfect beauty, uniquely expressed through you.

Write down the old beliefs you need to lay down to freely live from the beauty set within you. Feel free to write out your new beliefs.

PART 4

A Glimpse of the Brand New

Come out from them and be separate.
—2 Corinthians 6:17 NIV

With so many voices calling out to us, we can easily forget who we are and what our lives were meant to reflect. We can get caught up in the confusion and standards of this world, which makes it hard to see the new things that have been set out for us. We were never supposed to blend in or try to be someone else.

From the very beginning, God has called us to a royal position we never deserved. For some of us, it feels better to stay hidden. Others wind up stuck in the place of self-sabotage; they don't know how to get out. For others, our own success and recognition can be too costly to let go of. For some, our self-confidence appears to be the reason behind their success, wisdom, and beauty. The world shouts to us, "Do whatever it takes to be great. Just do you." And to that, God responds, "But we have this treasure in jars of clay to show that this all-surpassing power is from God and not from us" (2 Corinthians 4:7 NIV). We need this constant reminder that our ordinary outer shell is only a small part of who we are, while the world continues to tell us that this visible part of us is all we have. To be separate doesn't mean we are better or higher, but it does call us to live by a different standard, a heavenly one, one that brings both royalty and restraint.

THE BEAUTY IN YOU

When you and I were made in our mother's womb, we were marked with beauty, perfect beauty. No matter what happened to us in our life or what we look like, this still holds true. It is an amazing and powerful truth about us. The world, instead, says *you,* in fact, are the object of beauty and lures you to work harder to keep it. Keep striving, showing more, and setting better goals to get there for all to see. But when you look at your created purpose, this was not assigned to you. You were meant to reflect the beauty that is already wired deep inside of you. If you try and compare it to someone or something else, it becomes unsatisfying.

> **You were meant to reflect the beauty that is already wired deep inside of you.**

The truth is, no one is prettier, no one is more valuable than another because nothing in this world can compare. We are all an expression of God's great masterpiece. It is not based on a mold; no filter can enhance it. Therefore, you don't become beautiful because of what someone says or doesn't say about you or how beautiful you try to make yourself. There is a brilliance already in you, and it's far greater than any platform or selfie. Look at the fingerprints of the Creator on your hands and feet, the visible reminder that there is only one of you.

A few years ago, Dove had a campaign asking women in countries around the world what they thought of themselves based on which door they chose to walk through. One door read "Average," and the other read "Beautiful." The results sparked much attention. Over 95 percent of the women walked through the Average door, launching the movement for women to rethink how they saw themselves. The #choosebeautiful campaign was born so more women would think of themselves as beautiful. It is safe to say that the essence of beauty and value is not just a part of one culture, but in fact every culture.

Sandra L. Coates

THE DIAMOND DEPOSIT

I love the tagline "Diamonds are a girl's best friend." It speaks of how women are wired, without even trying. Don't we all want to be rare, precious, glowing, and chiseled? If you read about diamonds, you can trace them back thousands of years. They have always been considered one of the most admired and brilliant stones on earth. According to geology.com, "Diamonds form from pure carbon in the mantle under extreme heat and pressure." The word *diamond* originates from a Greek word that means "unconquerable." This suggests the ultimate nature of love, further going along with the Greek philosophy that the fiery brilliance of the diamond reflects the "undying flame of love" (diamondrocks.co.uk).

Diamonds have different cuts that reflect when light hits them. Jewelry experts say "every diamond is unique" and "no two diamonds are alike" (www.gia.edu). Just like you and me, and every human who has ever lived, there are no two alike. Their unique detail is an expression of the God who puts His design in you and me for a specific purpose: to reflect the many facets of His beauty.

The world tries to convince us that we are the image to watch, and therefore, we need to be flawless, like a diamond. The problem with this mentality is that we were never created to be the object of beauty; rather, we were meant to bear the reflection of ultimate and perfect beauty. It's amazing to think that this beautiful treasure lives inside of each of us. We all have this deposit of exceptional beauty and worth in us, but we are in the refining process. If you look at how a true diamond is formed, you will see it actually originates from material in the earth that becomes its full expression, only after much time and extreme heat and pressure. We don't start out as a finished work, all polished and sparkly; we need to develop and mature, just like the diamond.

We fail to recognize the need for all types of beauty. No one is better or prettier than another. All are unique and are exquisitely, equally beautiful. Like no two fingerprints or diamonds are alike, we are all hardwired to display a brilliance that no one has ever seen before. God made us to bear this image, and absolutely nothing is more beautiful than the One Who created us. We are worth so much more than we know.

| WE ALL HAVE THEM

One of the most powerful and often misunderstood truths about us are the battle scars we all hold. For some, this may be based on outward flaws or visible imperfections. While for others, this is based on a traumatic event, a season, or perhaps a diagnosis you have gone through. Big or small, they are real, and they are a part of our story. Whether visible or unseen, active or in the past, they tell of a bigger story happening that we often can't see or articulate.

God knows every one of these stories; He knows where we fight or hide, and He wants to meet us there. The pain and burdens we have faced are not forgotten but rather lovingly and carefully tended to by a heavenly Father, Who knows each and every piece of our story better than we ever could. When we invite Him into these places and bring our scarred selves, something changes. He walks with us, bringing His comfort and His rest to what we ourselves could not experience on our own. Over time, we see markings of heavenly strength and perfect love colliding with our imperfect story. "Those who live in the shelter of the Most High will find rest in the shadow of the Almighty" (Psalm 91:1 NLT).

We must not forget there is another One known for His scars. His name is Jesus, and He, God's Son, came to this earth to redeem the world with His own life and body, to overcome sin and pain and death. His nail-pierced hands, His crown of thorns, and the stripes on His body testify of a grander beauty that brought the ultimate redemption for all of humanity. He knows pain and suffering like no other human has ever faced.

His powerful beauty was at the pinnacle when He rose to heaven, after all the prophecies came true and He was nailed to a cross through the ultimate suffering and death. He sees exactly where we are and knows the battles we are fighting because He has gone before us, and it is there that He stands with us. "He was pierced for our transgressions, he was crushed for our sin; the punishment that brought us peace was on him, and by His wounds we are healed" (Isaiah 53:5 NIV). The pain He endured on our behalf shouts of our great worth.

What if we looked at our wounds and our scars with this same perspective? This view shows that nothing can take away our beauty and the victorious battle our lives testify to. What if through all of our pain and battle wounds on this journey, our identity is held in the hands of Jesus, the greatest model of beauty there is? This is the invitation of hope we are given to partake of this heavenly freedom, here and now. No matter where we have been, we are, in fact, the recipients of the greatest rescue there ever was.

> **No matter where we have been, we are, in fact, the recipients of the greatest rescue there ever was.**

A VISION OF BEAUTY

One morning years ago, I was running on the treadmill at the gym with my headphones on full blast, lost in the beat. There were several people there, all focused on their workouts. On the TV screen directly in front of me, there was a story about new fashion trends. I, being a fashionista at heart, began to pay attention. I watched woman after woman walk down a fancy runway featuring the newest collection, with lots of cameras and front-row spectators watching their every move. They all appeared to look very similar in color, size, and expression. They were noticeably thin, and the oversized clothes seemed to just swallow up their bodies.

I knew I was not an expert in fashion industry standards, but I could not help but ask some questions. Why did it all look so flat? Why did everyone look the same? The models looked miserable, so gaunt and serious on the runway. I never saw one person crack an expression, let alone a hint of a smile. As I was finishing my workout, I kept thinking something was just not right. The way it was presented lacked vibrance and culture and life. Despite all the time and money invested in this big event, I didn't want to watch it.

I imagined fashion to be exciting and celebrated in a way that matches the vibrant colors, spirits, and curves of everyday women. I started to dream about the what ifs: What if we had a fashion show featuring all kinds of women, from all different backgrounds, who illuminated the runway with their unique size, culture, age, and joy from the Lord? The clothes would light up because the women wearing them were full of God's beauty. It stirred something in me that would lie dormant for many years, but one day, it came to life.

After years of a desire in my heart to build a new organization, UNITED + TRU was born. UNITED + TRU (**T**ransformed. **R**edeemed. **U**nique) reaches women and girls of all ages, races, sizes, and backgrounds, showcasing the beauty in each and every girl that no one else holds. It's about reflecting the ultimate picture of beauty that God designed and remembering that we weren't made to look like anyone else. You and I were made for a glorious and specific purpose that far exceeds any goal or influential position we can come up with.

UNITED + TRU is about one body experiencing freedom and redefining beauty for each and every woman. What the world has tried to divide, segregate, and label as beautiful, God has declared otherwise. Together, we stand as a uniquely beautiful community, encouraging more and more women to find their voice and watch how much more lives in them. Our first big event was a huge fashion show, with empowering speakers and exclusive designers featuring local women and girls as runway models. The lobby was filled with local vendors and a photobooth to glam it up. The vision that God had given me previously became a real, live moment; so many women and girls were able to unite and share in it. It was more than just a fashion show or a girls' night out. It was a stage made for a bigger movement, with more women experiencing the beauty within them and the community of women around them. A spark was ignited in each and every heart.

Some of the role models in the show shared their experiences:

> When I was asked to be a role model for the fashion show, I was nervous; but when I noticed all the different ages, body shapes, and skin colors that were being represented, I felt so free. It is exactly how I imagine heaven to be! It was so exciting to be a part of a fashion show whose goal was to showcase how God created our bodies uniquely beautiful. He … gives us hearts and souls that are meant to radiate with His glory! (Ellie)

> I often say, God can take my mess and make it a message. I was blown away by the amazing women in the show and behind the scenes. I pulled up and saw all these beautiful women and questioned myself. The voices of my past began to taunt me. But, as I walked in and encountered the amazing love, the voices were silenced. On the night of

the fashion show, I was determined that, no matter what, I would shine and glorify my Father and thank Him for making me as He did. Each step was a statement of faith and thankfulness to Him. My little granddaughter was nervous, but I got to share with her that she had a gift no one else had. She looked at me and said, "Let's do this then!" She thought, as all of us do, she had to be perfect like the world's image, but God sees each of us in our unique beauty as a gift to the world. The enemy wants to hold us back and have us hide our gift. We defeat him when we share the gift of God in us with this hurting world! (Debra)

Practicing standing in the mirror in my heels and pajama pants made me remember the girl I was before: free-spirited, but afraid of the darkness of the world, of experiences she would never be able to talk about. She was a lovely bird in an iron cage of guilt and fear. Oh, but she survived; she pushed through incredible pain and continued to love people, even when it was hard. She became me. I posed. And it felt strong. This time, I was able to stand with and for women who had been girls like me and girls who will grow to be stronger than I ever will! This time, I didn't just walk down the runway. Finally uncaged, I believe I flew. (Trey)

Immediately after the show, the auditorium cleared out, but the runway was still lit, and the lights were on. The younger girls who had been guests at the show were playing around and decided to do their own runway walk. As they each proudly walked the runway, smiling, the other girls began to cheer them on and encourage them. It was as if the fire was lit, and the flame was being passed on. This is the way it was meant to be.

All along, God purposed us to be image bearers of His beauty, like a brilliant diamond. We, however, are not diamonds; rather, we were made to be a gorgeous reflection of Him. His unstoppable light and radiant beauty call out our worthiness.

What if instead of us following the world and the culture with its form of beauty, it started to follow us? What if women began to see clearly their unique beauty that has always been within them and have it spread like wildfire to every woman? Isn't that where freedom is?

UNITED FAR AND WIDE

UNITED + TRU also supports organizations, both locally and worldwide, fighting to end human trafficking in the world. A21, an organization founded by Christine and Nick Caine. A21, or "Abolish in 2021" along with Safe House Project are some of those groups who are fighting to rescue and restore those without hope and without a voice. Their staff works with local authorities and goes where brothels and illegal sex-trafficking operations are happening to free these precious victims. We want to join them in their mission to end human trafficking by financially giving a portion of our event proceeds.

FREEDOM

> I freed thousands of slaves. I could have freed thousands
> more, if they had known they were slaves.
> —Harriet Tubman

Isn't freedom what we all want? Unrestrained, to be authentically and confidently who we're made to be. Sounds amazing, right? To be set free is the ultimate gift.

As you probably know by now, it doesn't take much for us to find ourselves bound up. Part of the challenge is recognizing when we are not living free. If we want to experience freedom, we need to first know what bondage is and recognize our tendency to drift there. God clearly tells us that we are called to be His chosen people, and that includes freedom from all that attempts to enslave us. God made freedom possible through Jesus, as we exchange all of our sin and shame and suffering for His righteousness. We are no longer slaves to sin because we have been set free; our chains have been cut, once and for all. He made that possible and available for our taking.

"So if the Son sets you free, you are free indeed" (John 8:36 NIV).

Ultimately, freedom is not about getting what you want but rather what has been paid for you to have. God offers us His healing and forgiveness, and when we partake of it, freedom begins to flow. Freedom doesn't come when life is going well and we've made it. Real and true freedom comes when you and I no longer try to live from setting ourselves free because we have taken hold of a better freedom.

In the freedom God offers, you no longer have to worry about what the world thinks. It is a gift, not bound up by your own ideas or rules. When you try to be in charge of finding your own freedom, you fall short. Only through God's amazing grace and the finished work of Jesus can you find true and lasting freedom. This kind of freedom, no one can take away from you. Those who tried to defeat you or hold you captive are powerless. We are reminded of the incredible, brand-new identity that comes forth as we lay our old self down. The Bible says, "Therefore if anyone is in Christ, they are a new creation. The old has gone, the new has come" (2 Corinthians 5:17 NIV).

We become a walking picture of God's freedom as we surrender our lives to His incredible gift of salvation through Jesus. It's more than just a second chance; it's a brand-new start, with lasting hope for so much more. It's just that good.

EVERY WOMAN ON THE RUNWAY

When I think about beauty contests and fashion shows, my mind goes to pageants, gowns, competition, and lots of skin showing. I think Hollywood style, with limos, cameras, and crowds. I think about top models and magazine covers and the outwardly perfect formula of a woman. I can only begin to understand the work that goes into all of this. The focus remains on who looks the best, walks the best, and wins the hearts of the most judges and influencers. After the show is over, you see it in magazines and on social media platforms. Although so much good can occur, it's open season for ratings and comments on who nailed it and who didn't. If you stop and think about it, it's really what is bred in us as women: Fight to win the beauty contest to see who gets the crown.

But this war for our beauty is not against one another. It is about our God-breathed, God-ordained value and royal position, and an enemy who knows this truth as well and would love to try everything possible to steal it away. We are all daughters of the King. Just because we age, or we sin, or we doubt and fall away, that doesn't change His claim over us. Our life has the potential to be a fresh new start each and every step of the way. Only a perfect love, a holy presence, and a real and faithful God could activate that change. It is for every culture, every race, every age, and every story.

The culture we live in is frantically trying to control the darkness that lurks around.

There is another work at hand, on an active mission to be radiant, beautiful, adored, powerful, self-reliant, self-promoting, and in control. We, the adopted and chosen daughters of Christ, are invited to know this; we are reminded of a brand-new identity that comes forth as we lay our old selves down.

There is only ever one of you. You reflect the image of the perfect One. Therefore, negative self-talk, comparison, perfectionism, competition, and being embarrassed by your size, appearance, or family holds no ground. You are a rare and precious gift to the world.

MODELS NEEDED

At some point in their lives, the thought of being a model crosses most girls' minds. They imagine getting all dressed up like a celebrity and walking confidently across a stage while people fight to take pictures and make a big deal. We role-play in front of our mirrors, practice poses and smiles, make videos, and take selfies. We want to be noticed, feel special, and act confident. We want to be among the elite few, to feel and look amazing. This desire is wired in us. The truth is, we are defined, but the roles we play don't define us. Wired in each of us is a much bigger inheritance that offers more than what this life on earth has to offer.

In this world, we are in desperate need of models. I'm not talking about the beautiful ladies who get paid by agencies, or don the covers of magazines with smiles, or strut down runways with confidence. Their work is to provide eye-catching images that get attention, gain influence, and sell products. It's their job, not everyday, real life.

What we are in need of is role models we can look up to and draw strength from. We all know someone like this. These are young and old women who are not held back by their imperfections, failures, or insecurities. They stand out because they see others through the same glow they have themselves. They reflect a light and a joy that can't be matched. They have faced adversity, they have been in the trenches, and they have chosen to not live life in their own strength. It's not a focus of being the best, but rather a choice to take hold of the greatness that overflows from within. It is being intentional about who is watching and what they can learn about the glow inside of them.

If you want to be something great, be a role model. Girls are watching and following: brand-new moms, coworkers, students, singles, churchgoers, atheists, and everyone in between. Your friends are most influenced by who you are, how you live, and what you say and choose not to say. Are you focused on all your shortcomings and imperfections? Do you talk more about what you're not and compare yourself to someone else? Are you so hard on yourself that making mistakes is unacceptable? Or are you living in the freedom set out just for you? Nothing will kill your joy and passion to walk with others more than to stay focused on yourself.

Who you are has been fashioned uniquely and wonderfully by God, for you to live out together with Him. You are leaving a legacy, and you don't need a platform or a microphone to achieve that. As a leader for Christ, you already have influence. Something as simple as what we choose to wear, the self-control over our speech, the joy in our spirit, or the forgiveness we offer speaks volumes. Let us stand out for choosing to take the narrow road rather than following the crowd (see Matthew 7:13–14).

Our souls are hungry for more than this world has to offer. We have to choose to live like ones waiting for the grand finale in heaven on the other side.

Our souls are hungry for more than this world has to offer.

One woman, Katherine Wolf, lives this out every day she is alive. This former model suffered a massive stroke and traumatic brain injury at age twenty-six, just months after giving birth to her first son. She now speaks about the power of God, with scars, recovering speech, and a forever changed soul. Her message is both powerful and challenging to hold onto hope. She and her husband Jay now minister to others out of the suffering they endured. In their book, *Hope Heals*, Katherine writes, "Don't wait to celebrate the life you've been given, even if it looks different from the one you thought you'd have." Together, they offer a Christ-centered hope through their books, podcasts, and camps to help so many others. Her compelling spirit of hope and joy captures beauty beyond a magazine cover. She is a visible example of a beautiful role model and a true warrior in God's army, fighting on the battlefield.

Our legacy is not about what we can build or avoid or achieve; it's about our surrendered position to a holy God who has appointed assignments for you and I to do. It's never what you can accomplish in your own power. He signs His name on our lives with the miraculous, the humanly inconceivable, and the redemptively glorious things as we stand surrendered. That is our God.

THE RACE WE ARE RUNNING

We're in a race, and we are running towards something. Some of us may be more aware of that than others because we're feeling the pressure of age, or we're at a crossroad. But we all are still in the race. In her book *Unstoppable*, Christine Caine writes about this race, this destiny or assignment we have all been given. She refers to the divine baton that we are all carrying in this race and who we are becoming through running and not giving up: "Carrying the baton in our race is never about what *we* can accomplish *for* God. If he wanted, God could accomplish everything on his own without us. … As you continue in your race, refuse to focus on what you are not, what you cannot do, and what you do not know. Rely on God's power. Rely on God's resources. Rely on God's ways."

I want to run the race marked out for me. This doesn't stop when I don't get into the college I want, or get married by a certain age, or achieve certain letters behind my name. It's not whether my kids turn out the way I thought, or my marriage is on the rocks, or I'm still waiting for the love of my life to show up. The race is here, and you're in it.

Caine also writes, "I don't know what your past is. I don't know what pains or sorrows or sins you carry. But I do know that God can turn all of it around and use your past to give someone else a future. That's what Jesus does. The divine relay is all about passing the baton from one life to another, from one generation to the next."

So much of our part is about picking up the appointed baton and running our race. To do this, we need to believe that we have been given a critical part to play and anticipate the greater things that lie ahead. We need to pay attention to that want for something more and not try to silence it.

I don't know what has tried to disqualify you, but it cannot compare to the victory you have been graciously given by Jesus Christ. All of us in our brokenness remain in desperate need of the unmerited favor and mercy of His finished work for us. Why do we try and puff ourselves up and showcase ourselves, as if we're not in over our heads? Our wounds and sins are often displayed in beautifully wrapped packages of humanness. Jesus abolished shame with His very entry into humanity, born to a teenage girl in a dirty stable, until he took His last breath, suffering on a wooden cross at Calvary.

We've got to decide what side we stand on. It really comes down to our roots; what is our foundation built on? It's what gives us confidence, not in the outcome, but in Who we belong to. If we put God first, if we claim His favor and goodness, and if we say we are a Christian and therefore follow Christ, then our life will look different. We must accept that we are heirs of the greatest King and have been given a gracious inheritance. We must yield to our desires to be on the throne. We must accept that the Bible is God's spoken Word, inspired through human writing, and it is for us to follow and allow it to change us.

The Holy Spirit is real; He speaks and counsels with truths that align with God's Word to move in us and make us more like Jesus. We all need supernatural wisdom and counsel. We can't sprinkle God into our lives. We can't throw His name around and not surrender ourselves in worship to His holy and perfect name. We also can't continue in the same rut, calling ourselves negative names or categorizing ourselves as uninvited, not acceptable, or not lovable. Accepting that we are His beautiful masterpiece comes with humility and faith, not of our own doing and not for our own glory. We are part of something much bigger.

Above all, don't downplay your story, where you've come from, or your gifts. So many women think they need to get a better story or grow in knowledge or experience or whatever before they can be used for great things. There is nothing further from the truth. God is the One Who takes your exact story as it is and makes it beautiful, powerful, and transforming. You don't have the kind of supernatural power to make that happen. He needs you to come, empty-handed and hungry for more than what you can see. The adventure awaits, if you're ready.

> **Above all, don't downplay your story, where you've come from, or your gifts.**

What does He need to do this?

All of you, every broken piece, every award-winning piece, yielding to His plan and learning to trust every minute of your life that He will fulfill His promise to never leave you. He came down from heaven to rescue a people full of themselves and their sin; He showed us the greatest love this world has never known. It's the greatest love story because you were worth rescuing. You were the chosen one, the leading lady in the story.

So don't worry: He can handle your questions, your anger, your fears, and the walls you put up. He is your safety and your refuge. He speaks of the opportunities He has for you that He planned before He called you into being. The plans He has for us are really, as He says, "plans to prosper you and not to harm you, plans to give you hope and a future" (Jeremiah 29:11 NIV).

COMMUNITY

Every woman of every age and season wants to fit in. It's not just for school-aged girls, a popularity contest, or who throws the best parties. It is the real, genuine, deep need to feel like you're accepted and belong. We know this dynamic all too well when we see the endless steps taken by women to be included and the impact on them when they are not. Whether it is to be asked into a sorority, find the right playgroup, be invited to a special event, feel part of a conversation at church, have a place at the lunch table, or not just be the one who hosts or ministers to others, it is a huge deal for us as women. When we feel like we belong, with no prerequisite attached, there is a shifting inside. We come alive. This is definitely proof that we all have longings that need filling. There is a natural desire, placed in us by God, to be in community with others and, more importantly, with Him.

THE LIFELINE OF SISTERS

Where would I be without the lifeline of sisters who spoke into the pain and hopelessness of the space I was in? It usually starts with, "I don't want to complain but …" I often confuse complaining with speaking about the reality of what's tripping me up at the moment and trying to taunt me with defeat. These women in my life speak truth and offer fresh air that I am gasping for in those moments. They are sisters and saints, and sometimes even strangers, who give you light in the darkness and hope that you can see at a distance. It's the perfect timing of a text message checking on you or reminding you of a Bible verse, or a bystander's compliment on a day when you have nothing good to say, or an invite from a new friend who wants you to sit next to her at church. It is the time when a mentor shares her deepest regret of parenting as she looks back over those days that you are currently living. As she listens to your busy flood of daily struggles and emotions of trying to do it all well, she shares, "You can't do it all. God has to fill in the gaps."

Her comment allows you to take a deep breath, sink back into your chair, and feel the soothing balm of her words over your exhausted mind and heart. She gives you back your beauty and worth as a mom, regardless of the thankless moments and years of serving. Now you can see the framework of your assignment apart from all the mundane, tiring moments, the gray hairs, and the feeling of being inadequate.

TOGETHER, WE MUST RISE

One of our deepest needs, and yet one of our greatest fears, is to admit that we need each other. It's a risk to be vulnerable and put yourself out there in friendship. When friendship is like a sisterhood, it is worth every risk, but the road is never seamless, without bumps and scrapes or even falling-outs that don't end well.

We are made to be in community, to belong, to look out for one another, and to be strategic in our efforts. It has been that way since the beginning. Women have gathered together, prepared meals, planned parties and service projects, and gone out for a girls' night or just a cup of coffee; good gracious, we even go to the bathroom in groups. When we feel safe, there is nothing better than being in a tribe among other women.

The stakes can get pretty high when it comes to the power of community. Get a few ladies together who feel a connected strength and fierce power to conquer a mission, and it's a wonderful chain of events. They become one mind: focused, on point, and dialed in to accomplishing the mission and opposing their enemies. No longer is the focus about comparing, competing, judging or winning. Instead, beauty emerges as one collective, dynamic team together. They feel purpose, they draw strength, they pray on behalf of one another, and they have a place to belong.

In Lisa Bevere's book *Lioness Arising*, she gives a different perspective on females working together for the good of others; she studied lions and lionesses in their natural habitat and the inner workings of their success in the animal kingdom. She writes, "Let us be 'dangerously awake' like the lioness knowing who we are with the power inside of us to conquer giants and come to the rescue of our fellow sisters. Rest in Him, relax with one another and together be ferocious in the face of darkness."

SHOUTOUT TO THE SINGLE LADIES

We were all created for close relationships. That was, and is, God's plan. We often confuse closeness with dating, marriage, or having a family with children. Feeling like you've arrived as a woman seems to include these mile markers along the journey. As I hear from many single friends, and as I remember myself, there is a deep longing to have someone to go through life with. As time goes on and windows of opportunity begin to close, it can be so hard to hope for more. As one of my single friend says, "It's downright lonely sometimes as a single woman, looking at everyone's life that seems to be moving on while yours is standing still. I kept giving myself away because I didn't know my worth. All along, He assigned worth to me with no strings attached. Hold on, sisters; more is coming. Believe in your worth. Stand firm in your faith. God sees you, and He will bring more."

> **There is something about being chosen that is what we all long for and what every one of us needs to hear.**

Jesus says, "You did not choose me, but I chose you" (John 15:16 NIV). There is something about being chosen that is what we all long for and what every one of us needs to hear. It's as if God was saying, "I know you, because I made you, and I know you were made for community, to be liked and accepted and seen and heard and treated with value and specific purpose. I, God, am the One who sees you. Make no mistake: I also know the deepest and darkest parts about you, and I still choose you and accept you every time. I will never reject you or abandon you. Out of this you will rise and be filled and give this gift away to others. That is where your confidence and security and happiness will flow from, and you will be satisfied."

"You open your hand and satisfy the desires of every living thing" (Psalm 145:16 NIV).

Notice the enormity of that claim and who He says will satisfy us. He doesn't mention anyone or anything else besides Himself. So if He sees us, knows us, and wants us to be satisfied, then why do we go seeking everywhere else for what only He promises to do? Love has never been more on your side, more available, more freeing, and more satisfying, than with a covenant relationship offered from God.

May we take the time to get to know His ways and His thoughts and let them shape our identity, our worth, and become our source of satisfaction.

TO EVERY GIRL OUT THERE

We need to build one another up and out of that build trust with one another. We as women were made to be relational, to be in a community that spurs one another on but so often we tear one another down. You can be as different as they come: introverted and shy, or extroverted and loud. We can be sweet and innocent, a wide-open book and transparent, tough as nails appearing there is no vulnerable side. We all need God's Word and grace-filled truths over us to train us and help us mature and grow. But as different as we can seem, we all have an underbelly underneath the exterior that is capable of being hurt and disappointed and longs for safe places to land in relationships. You and I were still made to need each other, help each other and forgive each other. When we cheer one another on in this journey, rather than sit in judgment, it brings out a new confidence we otherwise just wouldn't have. To not be threatened by one another's gifts, beauty or position evens the playing field and creates a safety net where respect and admiration can be freely given and received.

HER VERY BEST

It all happened so quickly, and there was nothing I could do about it. Right before my eyes, I broke a really expensive bottle of essential oil on my kitchen countertop. I looked down and saw the hundreds of glass shards intermixed with my coveted blend of fragrant liquid, dripping off the edge. As I started thinking of how I could possibly salvage this precious liquid, the story of the woman with the alabaster jar came to mind. Mary of Bethany was her name, and she knew about this Jesus far better than most. He had captured her heart, and she chose to give Him all she had.

> Now one of the Pharisees invited Jesus to have dinner with him, so he went to the Pharisee's house and reclined at the table. When a woman who had lived a sinful life in that town learned that Jesus was eating at the Pharisee's house, she brought an alabaster jar of perfume, and as she stood behind him at his feet weeping, she began to wet his feet with her tears. Then she wiped them with her hair, kissed them and poured perfume on them. When the Pharisee who had invited him saw this, he said to himself, "If this man were a prophet, he would know who is touching him and what kind of woman she is, that she is a sinner." (Luke 7:36–39 NIV)

She didn't hesitate to break open her one and only coveted jar of perfume and give it all away to Him. As she bowed in reverence and kissed his feet in front of everyone, she was overcome. Wiping the excess perfume and tears with her hair, the boldest of love and affection came alive. She couldn't wait to give all she had away to Jesus. She brought her greatest possession and gave all of herself that day. She didn't care who was watching or what the consequences were. His love for her was captivating, and she felt full for the first time. She, a fellow warrior, saw a glimpse of greatness of who she was because of His power and love for her. Giving away her greatest possession and the battle scars she would endure from it was worth every moment of risk; she gave herself to the only One who is worthy to receive it all.

Jesus went on to be her defender; He protected her from the accusations made about her sin in front of all the leaders. He didn't bring up her past but instead celebrated her boldness of love in the face of shame and rejection. She had never felt so safe and full of hope in her life; He had seen her as a gift, not as an object, a possession, or a disappointment. He had taken on her humiliation, and she tasted freedom. Giving away her perfume jar was worth it all; He ended with this defense: "Her many sins have been forgiven, for she loved much. Jesus said to the woman, 'Your faith has saved you; go in peace'" (Luke 7:47, 50 NIV). She left there changed because of the cleansing gift of forgiveness she had received; her past no longer had a hold over her. She was free now to radiate the beauty that had always been inside of her. It was only the beginning of a new start, even if the culture hadn't changed.

Jesus calls us worthy, He sets our paths straight, He covers us with his righteousness, and He cleanses us from all of our costly mistakes. He is our Rescuer; He brings us alive.

FOREVER CHANGED

Psalm 40:1–3 (NIV) says, "I waited patiently for the Lord to help me, and he turned to me and heard my cry. He lifted me out of the pit of despair, out of the mud and the mire. He set my feet on solid ground and gave me a firm place to stand. He put a new song in my mouth, a hymn of praise to our God. Many will see what he has done and be amazed. They will put their trust in the Lord."

Over the years, I have been asked what verses from the Bible explain my life. My answer is always Psalm 40. I didn't know at the time how to express what God did in me, but these verses articulate what I cannot say. For many years, I was so unsteady and self-centered, driven by worry and popularity that I couldn't even understand why someone would choose to follow God. It seemed either rule driven, rigid, radical, or overdone; if I'm really honest, it didn't seem necessary. I had no idea that God would want to seek me out in the pit of despair, that He would one day choose to use me as His beacon of light and hope for others. How could it be? I still fall into idol worship over food and self-loathing. I fight demons in my head that say I don't have what it takes, or that I need to work harder to stay young and earn my worth. I still fight jealousy and try to please people to win their approval and feel like I belong. I still have seasons of anxiety where I need medication to keep me balanced. I fear getting old and being alone or being left. To this day, I've never experienced having a daughter of my own, but the longing is still there.

You see, it's never over. The war still rages on, and the need for solid ground and absolute truth grows with each day. My mind is a battlefield, and it holds so much power, both for victory and destruction. You see, it's never the first episode of doubt that leads us astray or causes us to question God's goodness. It may start with a whisper or a difficult situation, but it often grows into much more. For example, I might choose not to go to a high school reunion or pool party; I may not want to be in a group picture because of how I look or what others might think or say of me. We become obsessed with how we look and how we compare to everyone else, rather than enjoying the experience set before us. The false message here is how we look or appear determines our worth and how valuable we are to others. If we continue to believe this, we will not see the special assignments carved out just for us. To move forward means we have to trust God, where we can't see who we really are and the beautiful impact we have to share with the world.

THE INVITATION FOR ALL

The heart and soul of God's beauty on display is showing off His creation of all races, ages, stages, and cultures. The ministry UNITED + TRU began as a movement to help women and girls band together to redefine beauty. We want to help women discover the way we are supposed to see ourselves and talk together about the issues and pressures we face. The heart of this mission is to showcase God's beauty in every woman, united as one body—every shape, size, age, and culture. Romans 8:28 (NIV) says God makes "all things work together for our good." He is able to take all the insecurities, pain, blemishes, and shame and use them for good to transform us into His beauty and light. He's a God of ultimate makeovers, changing women from the inside out—no filters needed.

You and I have been given an invitation to a relationship that will change our lives forever. You'll know if you have been because you won't be the same. You'll feel freer, full of amazing joy and love, more than you ever have before. It can happen anytime, usually when you least expect it. You may be tempted to see yourself as too far gone or too messed up and broken. This is exactly where God meets you and offers you an invitation to surrender all of it to Him in exchange for freedom and cleansing, where you won't carry your sins anymore. You stand behind the greatest Warrior who ever lived, who fights your battles and heals you. It's the greatest, most peaceful, and most satisfying kind of love you'll ever know. Through God's cleansing work in you each and every day (called sanctification), and the great Counselor, the Holy Spirit, you will have new eyes to see and a new hunger inside.

It really comes down to this: In order to believe in a God who claims sight for the blind and freedom for sinners, we have to abandon what we can't fathom with human reasoning and experience. We won't have the capacity to understand what the big deal is if we are convinced that we don't need a Savior, if we think we can do whatever we want on our own, if we try hard enough. This life with Jesus will always be countercultural. When we say yes to God, we are partnering with Him in divine ways, far beyond what we can comprehend or imagine. Your identity, who you are because of Christ, will become immovable, invincible to attack, and free from opposition.

So live out your story. It will never be anyone else's but yours. Every day we are here, our story continues to be told. Don't just buy the powerhouse words on a shirt; believe them. Live them with the strength and confidence that is far beyond your mere accomplishments. Don't hide yourself behind goals that impress but don't fulfill or be distracted by platforms or people that look great but leave you empty. Don't let someone else's words or criticism hold power over you; it's not theirs to hold. You are precious, you are fought for, your set of fingerprints can never be replicated, and neither can your irreplaceable life story. You have been made in the image of a God who has no match and whose power no one can stop. We need to accept that sometimes, we won't feel comfortable in our own skin, let alone feel like a warrior, but that doesn't mean we're not one. Over and over again, we will get the chance to be shown who we have always been. We need to keep asking, keep seeking, and keep believing that "greater is He that is in 'her', than He that is in the world" (1 John 4:4 NIV).

The goal is wholeness, the completed work that only a supernatural God can do in us. It's not about rising up to make the perfect goal list or find the right balance of self-confidence and worth. It's about His gracious acts of redemption on our behalf that reflect this work through our beautifully broken lives.

▍ WHO'S YOUR TREASURE?

We all want to be a part of something great, whether it's personal goals or making the world a better place by doing what hasn't been done before or being the change we want to see. It's taken over our thoughts, our careers, and our bank accounts. Yet we are often far too easily pleased to follow other people, other ideas, or other formulas we come up with in our heads, rather than a true and proven power source. When I was a little girl, I lived out my Wonder Woman superhero days, complete with costume, shiny gold belt, and a lasso. In my head, I was all power. But at the end of the day, there was no power, aside of me believing I was somebody bigger and better and stronger. It was a chance to dream of more (and an excuse to wear a really cool costume).

As we grow up, not much changes. We still want the power, but if we're honest, we don't want to use an outside source to get there or wait on anyone else. We struggle with a power source that doesn't work on our timetable and requires us to face our humanness, our sin nature, and our dependence on Him. Let's face it; it's just not attractive or comfortable. If you know about great leaders, they are marked with purpose, drive, and humility as they take others where they are going to make them great. Or are they?

If we look back, Jesus, the Son of God, was a celebrity in His day. Wherever He was speaking, preaching, healing, or just hanging out, that was where the crowds were. Some loved Him and immediately dropped everything to follow Him, while others hated Him and wanted to crucify Him. Regardless, there was something so majestic, so commanding, and so attractive about Him. If you look further at the life of Jesus, you see that women were especially drawn to Him because of how He saw them. It was unlike anything the culture had seen or done before, but their lack of rights and prestige were of no hindrance to this Messiah King. He called out their beauty and honored their worth in ways they could not put into words. As His time on earth came to an end, they would be the last ones at the cross where He was crucified and the first ones at the empty tomb where He had been laid. They had fallen in love with their Savior and would do whatever it took to be where He was.

There are many popular beliefs in today's culture that lead us to believe we humans are, in fact, the solution, the ones who hold the rewards to life and prosperity. We are the focus, the ones to follow, the ones in charge of our self-esteem, our self-worth, and our happiness. It can sound so good and feel so empowering to be in charge of your own destiny and not need anyone else. With all our impressive life coaches, mentors, and entrepreneurial skills, the opportunities are unlimited to what we can do to live a life of no apologies and self-made success.

But for all the times I've tried and wondered why I was failing, I realized I needed more than strength or ability, more than the grit of learning to choose happiness or fight for a better version of myself. In her book *Get Out of Your Head,* Jennie Allen explains, "We are not made to think more good thoughts about ourselves. We are made to experience life and peace as we begin to think less about ourselves and more about our Creator and about others. Self-help can offer only a better version of yourself; Christ is after a whole new you. God in you."

Throughout history, humans of every race and culture have wrestled with who the treasure really is. In other words, who or what is our object of worship? The truth is, you and I aren't the answer, and we never will be. Oh, there is one with the answer, and it's better than we can imagine. It is the very essence of beauty: breathtakingly perfect. Maybe that is why we can never be enough, on our own. We were meant to need more, crave more. The apostle Paul, a leader among leaders, who is credited for writing many of the New Testament letters, speaks clearly about himself and what his efforts bring. He makes this discovery about himself: "I come with nothing, I boast about nothing except one thing; that is who I am because of the work of one greater." (reference 2 Corinthians 12:5-6 NIV) "For when I am weak, then I am strong" (2 Corinthians 12:10b NIV).

If we look back to the description of Satan, his beauty, his pride, and his focus on self are the driving forces that all lead back to him as the treasure. When we look deeper into our own selves, we can see the same threads, when we're tempted to stay focused on achieving the very best version of what we believe we should be, solely for the sake of ourselves. It can all sound so good and often right that we would be the ones to accomplish such a task.

God is the treasure. End of story. He is the only one worthy of such a title. He is the radiant one. He is perfect, without sin or failure, and one day soon, He is coming back to make all things right. Whether we recognize it or not, His identity in us is the reward we are looking for. We all need constant reminders that we are not the treasure. We are sinful, frail, and prone to wander away. As we yield ourselves to Him, we get to be the recipients of this glorious treasure and carry an undeniable glow about us.

It's a choice we get to make; it's not an automatic reaction for us. If we choose to live for Him, then we must lay down our earthly treasures and the things we hold so dear. Life will include both sacrifice and fullness, as we chase after an inheritance far beyond this world. We will be challenged and chastised for our decisions, and we will experience suffering along with great blessings out of our yes to Him. Our eyes will see with a different lens, and we will have a longing for more than this world can offer. We will realize that our hunger is not one that this life can satisfy.

As a woman who now experiences God's beauty and confidence within me, I know that a miraculous God came in and changed me forever. There is no other explanation. What I thought was the conclusion of my life

But despite feeling insecure, lonely, unattractive, or whatever else comes my way, I choose to power up, hold my weapons tight, and believe the resurrected story He invited me to live out as my story.

story was so far from the truth. The tides shifted, and I am marked more than ever by His goodness. That doesn't mean that I am not still a sinner, in desperate need of forgiveness and grace and patience from God. So often I can slip and forget that I am still in a daily battle for the identity I have been given and the God-appointed life I have been called to. It can feel like a roller coaster before I even leave the house. But despite feeling insecure, lonely, unattractive, or whatever else comes my way, I choose to power up, hold my weapons tight, and believe the resurrected story He invited me to live out as my story.

RISE UP

I want to know the living God, not just hear about Him or get glimpses of Him and be satisfied. I want to be used for His great work in the epic battle at hand.

So let us be reminded: Evil has not won. Darkness, fear, pain, loneliness, and failure have not won. Those things are real and still lurking, but they do not have a hold on us. We stand behind the greatest King, the valiant Warrior Who is leading our every step. He is our light and our vision. We must get behind Him, be ready to fight and believe God in us will finish the race to victory.

There is a good fight happening, and we are in it. We will finish well if we take our position. It's time we rise up and take our place as women and girls who are ready to run the race marked out for us. Our posture is firm, not because of us, but because of who's unshakable platform we live from. "And we, who with unveiled faces all reflect the Lord's glory, are being transformed into His likeness with ever-increasing glory, which comes from the Lord, who is the Spirit" (2 Corinthians 3:18 NIV).

THE TIME IS NOW

You and I were made to illuminate God's brilliant and beautiful light that is within us. We must tell other women and our younger generations there is a radiant fire inside them that nothing can extinguish. Although the enemy still lurks, he has been defeated. He would love for us to think this life is all there is or that you are not enough to be in the battle. The truth is, we have all been appointed to train for this very battle as one awakened force. It is God Who holds us up. He wants to fill us with more supernatural power, to stand firm as we fight to set more captives free.

You were made for this, made to live a life that has been transformed by God, made to be a role model for someone else, made to stand strong in battle and be a shining example of His beauty and light. We will still have unanswered prayers and questions that, if we sit too long thinking about, will rob us of the very joy we have been graced with to face the day. Let us not forget the heavenly paradise that awaits us on the other side of all of this. This place on earth and all that is wrapped up in it will soon disappear and be but a vapor. Let it be said that we believed in the unbelievable promises granted to us to live out here and fight for now.

"They were all commended for their faith, yet none of them received what had been promised. God had planned something better for us so that only together with us would they be made perfect" (Hebrews 11:39–40 NIV).

The world has not yet seen this audacious plan, which is far too big and magnificent for here.

Victory has been won, but for now, we must hold our weapons tightly in battle as we fight together.

See you on the battlefield, my fellow warrior.

EPILOGUE

One Last Story: My Christmas Wish

One Christmas night a few years ago, I was putting the finishing touches on the decorations in my house. It's rare that it's quiet in my house and that I'm alone. As a mom of three boys who love to wrestle and play, it stays quite lively and loud. Usually, I'm listening for the distinct cries that I know means someone is hurt rather than just the testosterone-laden roars and screams universal to the male species.

Several years earlier, I started putting up my own little Christmas tree that had been given to me by a special aunt who had passed away. It was full of some of my favorite ornaments, including all the breakable ones I could not have near adventurous little boys. I put the fragile glass jar ornament filled with tiny candy canes on one branch. It held a special place in my heart. My coworker had picked it out at the gift shop while she was with her grandson in the hospital. Next to it was a red felt Starbucks gift card holder that said the word "wish" in silver cursive letters. It had been empty for quite some time, but I liked it, and it brought to life the spirit of the Christmas season. For some reason, I looked at it differently this year. As I pulled it out of the shoebox and placed it on the tree, I began to think for a minute about my wish. What would I wish for if I could ask for anything? I thought of something light and fun, but soon my eyes began to fill with tears as the buried thought came to mind. I found a pen and paper, and wrote these secret words: "a little girl." I slipped it inside the holder and wrapped the silver strap in figure eights to seal it closed.

I couldn't believe it; I wrote it down like a little kid scribbles out a list for Santa. It was one step closer to daring to dream and ask for something so big, without feeling guilty or silly. It plagued me, feeling so very blessed with the three beautiful boys I already had, that I would ask such a thing. Why would God listen to that request? I felt selfish. Shouldn't I be counting my blessings and moving on? Did I even know what I was asking for? Why can't I be content and thankful for what I was already given? After all, it's a lot more than many people have. I should just keep quiet. But something happened that day that made me a little giddy and nervous inside. It felt really good to let my guard down and expose a deep part of me. I never thought anyone would see the note besides me, and when Christmas was over, it would just go back in a box and sit in the attic until next year.

You see, I never got that wish to be pregnant with a little girl. I honestly wasn't sure if there was any point to even wish, but it would always be a special reminder to me that no wish is ever wasted. It can seem so foolish to put yourself out there and ask. It often seems better to play it safe and not dream for more. After all, who wants to feel worse by exposing the very longings you've painfully wished for?

After Christmas was over that year and we were busy putting away the decorations, I paused as I came across that same red envelope once again, with the note still inside. As I laid it in the shoebox with the other special ornaments I kept for my little tree, I heard a small voice inside speak to me: *Sandra, you're the girl.*

I paused as my eyes darted around, looking to see if anyone else heard what I heard. What? What does that even mean? I began to ponder. I know I'm the only girl here in a house full of boys. This whole wish thing was just a fun little game, I thought.

"No, no, you're the girl, Sandra; you're the gift." The secret whisper went on to say, "The you that I see is the same girl your heart longs for. I am the One who wants to show you the treasure you are to both me and those around you, the gift you have been since I made you and I put my Spirit in you. And despite all the mistakes and regrets and things that were severed and broken and left you with deep scars, you're the girl."

I stood in disbelief, holding this red wish holder, not realizing the shocking new set of eyes I had just been offered to see. For all these years, I had belittled that girl. I saw all her flaws, the unfinished goals, the fears, and the destructive patterns that had plagued her. How could I live not feeling like I was not enough or too much: too tall, too sensitive, too scatterbrained, and terrified of rejection? I was a project, after all, not an answer to someone's wish.

But as time went on, I never forgot that day and the invitation to see the gift within me. I have been beautifully, and sometimes uncomfortably, reminded that I am exactly what God desires of me. When He looks at me, He sees breathtaking beauty and purpose. End of story. I've had to let go and take captive all the destructive thoughts that quickly seep into my mind of who I'm not and instead look through His amazing grace, calling out for me. I've learned to boldly ask Him to show me again and again how He sees me, to remind me of the unending love that still chases after me. It's not a question for the world or others around me to answer. Those sources will always come up short. As I walk this out, I find new confidence coming over me, an acceptance of who I am and a warrior-like strength flowing through me, ready to do battle for the King. Jesus says these words as a reminder of the great assignment wired in each of us: "You did not choose me, but I chose you and appointed you to go and bear fruit, fruit that will last" (John 15:16 NIV).

As I write this today, it is because I had to accept the gift of me if I have any hope of challenging you to do the same. You are exactly what God desired. Better said, you are the girl too. You are the gift. There is no one else who can move your heart and change the countenance of your soul like He can. He has unending love stored up, just for you. His eyes are on you because you are His masterpiece, and there is simply no one like you.

Reflection/Discussion

What about God's Beauty/Your Community/Your Role Models

Reflection:

What does it mean to know beauty has already been deposited in you?

How do you look at your scars (whether literal or symbolic) differently?

Where in your life do you want to experience freedom?

Why does God want us to be in community and fighting on behalf of one another?

Truth: We are all image bearers of the most beautiful One, the One Who invented beauty.

"Where the Spirit of the Lord is there is freedom. And we, who with unveiled faces all reflect the Lord's glory, are being transformed into his likeness with ever-increasing glory" (2 Corinthians 3:17–18 NIV).

Big Idea: What we see will always pale in comparison to what God sees in us. Our beauty and freedom come as we accept the invitation to believe we are a reflection of His perfect beauty, like a diamond. God wants to use all of your life and your battle scars to be a role model for others.

Is there anything stopping you from thinking you are a role model for others?

How will you live differently, knowing you're the girl, and there is none like you?

SANDRA'S FASHION TRICKS

My motto is, "Don't let your clothes rule you."

I've always loved fashion. If you know me, you know I love thrift stores and hand-me-downs; I tell all my friends, "Don't let your clothes rule you." Call me a rebel, but there is just a thrill of cutting and shaping my wardrobe to fit what looks pretty and flattering on me rather than being confined to the rules of how they should be worn.

From the time I can remember, I had an eye for it. My mom used to tease me that I was notorious for finding the most expensive item in a store, without even trying. Since I was young, fashion plates were my jam, and keeping an eye on the latest styles and trends was a must for me. I was never the popular girl, but I could dream up and sketch out what was popular. For much of my life, I didn't fit in because of my size, but somehow, fashion eased some of that for me. As a young girl, I loved going to my nana's house and dressing up in her fancy tweed skirts, high heels, hats, and jewelry. We had so much fun. The best part was sitting at her vanity in front of the big oval mirror and opening all the drawers of her jewelry box and trying on all the treasures. As I looked in that mirror at the finished look—my huge clip-on earrings squeezing my earlobes—I remember feeling like a real beauty queen. It was magical feeling, so free and lovely in this glammed-up version of me.

One of the challenges I faced was finding cool clothes that fit me. Years back, there were no exceptions for my body size, no trendy clothing lines for bigger girls. It was a label I could not escape and led to lots of tears, anxiety, and shame; I often wanted to hide. I had a problem with how my body looked, and it deeply affected how I saw myself. I listened to the culture, and I looked to others for my image. How could I be made in the image of God with a world that didn't have a mold for me to fit into?

Fashion seemed to help mask the wounded parts and soften the blows of relentless questions about what grade I was really in or why I was so big for my age. Underneath it all, when I looked at myself in the mirror, I really wanted to be someone else. I wanted to be that petite, pretty, confident girl who felt blissful in her own skin. At times, I felt like I had a disease that I just had to live with, and I didn't think God cared. I didn't know He can use anything for my good. Good thing I didn't know the end of my story.

The questions for all of us become, what if we dictated fashion as an outward expression of an inward beauty, instead of it dictating to us? Better yet, what if we could know our unique body type, skin color, and style were created for a beautiful purpose and live in the comfort of our own skin? What if looking and feeling our best was not only when we got all dressed up or were the perfect size but how we felt every day?

Many years later, I still love fashion. However, my whole belief system and image of myself is brand new because of a God who was not afraid to walk me through my shame, insecurity, and self-loathing. It's a forever dance we play, but He never gets tired of me and my whispers of the same doubts.

So if there is truly nothing more beautiful than God, and we are called to reflect that beauty, then maybe what the world really needs is what we already have. The truth is, we already possess all the beauty and confidence we need. It has been there since the beginning. If we believe that, then maybe—just maybe—we can choose to dictate fashion instead of it dictating to us.

▌MY FASHION TRICKS

Favorite jeans: I love fringing the bottom of a pair of jeans or making them look distressed or cut a slit in the knee. Scissors, tweezers, and safety pins can all add to the worn-in look. Lastly, to the fashion angels who invented the forgivable, stretchy waistband for button-up jeans, I want to shout your names from the rooftops, whoever you are. I love having birthed three babies, but I don't need the daily reminder from my midsection. Anybody know what I'm talking about?

Boots: If you have a pair of calf-length boots that you don't wear anymore but you still like, turn them into something new. Stain them or color them or take a pair of scissors and make booties out of them. I can't tell you how many compliments I've gotten on those honey-brown booties I made out of my ten-year-old boots from Rack Room.

T-Shirts: If you need a change with a shirt or you want it not to just hang on you, then grab your scissors and get to work. I cut the neckline out for a more breathable scoop neck, change the sleeve length, or cut the bottom off. You can make a fringe bottom or make a slit up the middle and tie it to make it cute and fun; the symmetry will slim your middle at the same time. You can also use bands to make an ordinary shirt have a fun shape around your waistline.

Dresses: I let out the hem, cut some of it off, and make it a long tunic or oversized shirt. I have tried all kinds of things and almost always love the results. If I cut off too much, I have to go the shirt route and maybe make a scarf out of the material too. I can definitely get scissor happy, especially if I haven't planned it out ahead of time. Sometimes, your mistakes really do turn into masterpieces.

Bottom line, I love being a woman. I love style, and I love it even more when it's from my own closet or a hand-me-down from a friend. The possibilities are endless.

So have fun, and girl, don't let your clothes rule you.

I can't wait to see your amazing creations on the runway one day soon.

ACKNOWLEDGMENTS

To Brett: I couldn't have done this new and scary mission without you by my side. Your love and encouragement challenged me to keep going, even when it was so hard. I am so grateful for you and the journey God has us on together. I love you, and I choose you.

To Sawyer, Blake, and Fisher: Thank you for your grace and love, looking over my shoulder all those times, asking me if I was finally done writing this book. I pray that Dad and I show you what it means to love and cherish women. May your future wives know their amazing beauty and unique purpose.

To Mom: You have always been my cheerleader and my number one fan. So many opportunities in my life have come because you believed in me and pushed me to try. Thank you for your ongoing love and selflessness. I have learned so much through you.

To Mima: Thank you for always believing in me and speaking such great encouragement of a God-sized vision for me. I give thanks for you.

To Jean and Megan: I am so thankful for how you have loved and supported me all along this journey. You make life fun, and all the laughs and memories we share are such treasures. I am blessed to have you both in my life.

To Sylvia: Thank you for sharing your heart for Jesus with me and modeling a Christ-centered life for all these years. I will never forget our many family memories together and the road trips to New York City.

To Dee, Mary, and Ruthie: I am so grateful for each of you and your sweet love and support. I am so thankful God made us family.

To Miss Mason, my first grade teacher: Thank you for modeling all the great things about being really tall.

To my tribe: Thank you for your friendship, your fervent prayers, and your love for me over the years. Each of you is a life-giving gift. You have challenged, encouraged, and supported me over the years, in ways you may never know.

To Vernicia Eure, Olivia Lewis, Rachel Chapman, Kristi Anderson, Maddie Hunter, Debbie Childs, Paige Coulter, Christine Robinson, Chandra Jarrett, Autumn Leggett, Shannon Elrod, Cindy Griffin, Tracy Johnson, Liz Corder, Rachel Closs, Whitney Forestner, Racheal Graybill, Chandra Jarrett, Courtney Jordan, Kim Bloecher, Amy Froese, Katie Hamilton, Jessica MacFarland, Laura Smith, Kristi Foerster, Jenn Hoiler, Jamie Carpenter, Kelsey Jenney, Lexi Shipp, Stephanie Clark, and Cherie Rundle.

To the UNITED + TRU team: Arjola Mullaj, Carrie Sanders, Ashlee Hawley, Trey Campbell, Erica Lane, Erin Vickrey, Tiffany Rogers, Angela McDowell, Fabine Bryant, Deb Stewart, Rita Campbell, Ellie Hanson, Debra Reniva, Katey Oldsen, Erin Thompson, Gracie Goodwin, Tiffany McClain, Mary &Ruthie Coates, Becky Van Valin, Katrina Askew, Saulo Ortiz, Robin Mayo, Roz Thompson, Dana Williams, Toby and Karen DeBause, Christine Bradshaw, Charlie and Margaret Pittman.

To Pastor Jane Evans of Influencers Church: Thank you, my fellow fashionista, for following the big God-dream to preach the Good News from a fashion runway to so many girls. To share in this mission from two continents is simply an honor.

To CPC and the Keim Centers: Your support of me in this great God-sized dream is humbling. I am beyond grateful to have grown up spiritually over these past fifteen years, working with and serving so many amazing women. I am so thankful for your leadership and encouragement to stay strong in the battle.

To Young Life VB South: Thank you for being such a cheerleader and a powerful encouragement to me and my family. Mike Terranova, Zed Meko, and Kristin Patterson, I'm honored to be in the mission field with you all, loving and reaching this generation together.

To AMTC family (NY/NJ Hub): You opened my eyes and made my heart swell with joy seeing the vast and unique talent of each performer. Carey Lewis, your faithfulness to this mission and your leadership have changed too many lives to count. I am inspired by you to never stop being a role model in this world.

To Real Life Christian Church: Thank you for your generosity and your love for Brett and me and our boys over the years. Your faithful and steadfast love for God's mission in our community has been such a blessing. We have weathered many storms, and together we rise. What an incredible building we have to hold our runway fashion show events.

To my content editor, Amanda Alix: Thank you for taking the leap to be in this wild journey with me. I am so grateful for your organized, detail-oriented mind and your grace for all my many word tangents and run-on sentences. Your gifted skill set on all those late Sunday nights, helping me bring this book to life, was an amazing experience.

To Sara Hagerty: Thank you for cheering me on and being a tangible inspiration in this scary and life-changing journey of book writing. Your books have ministered to me deep within and have challenged me to greater heights with God. I am grateful we met all those years ago at YL summer camp.

To some of my biggest heroes in the faith: Thank you, Beth Moore, Jada Edwards, Jennie Allen, Priscilla Shirer, Katherine Wolfe, Lysa TerKeurst, Stasi Eldridge, Jackie Hill Perry, and Christine Caine. Propel Women's Conference, She Speaks Conference, IF Gathering, and so many books and Bible studies have spurred me on and compelled me to keep going for more of God. Thank you for being brave and being a sacrificial role model for so many of us who are wondering if the God-sized dream inside of us is possible. You have paved the way.

Finally, to Lord Jesus: Only You could open the sacred space of my mind and take me through all the late nights and early mornings of writing and somehow bring me to the other side. I am humbled that You would choose to use my mess and make it a platform for something great. Your name is the greatest name there is, and Your love has no end. May You be glorified and lifted high through it all.

NOTES

Part 1

Bethany Hamilton quotes (bethanyhamilton.com).

Peter Scazzero, *Emotionally Healthy Spirituality: It's Impossible to Be Spiritually Mature while Remaining Emotionally Immature* (Grand Rapids, MI: Zondervan, 2017), p 12.

Jackie Hill Perry, *Gay Girl, Good God: The Story of Who I Was and Who God Has Always Been* (Nashville, TN: B&H Publishing Group, 2018), p 86.

Lysa TerKeurst, *Uninvited: Living Loved When You Feel Less Than, Left Out, and Lonely* (Nashville, TN: Thomas Nelson, 2016), p 51.

Jennie Allen, *Get Out of Your Head: Stopping the Spiral of Toxic Thoughts* (Colorado Springs, CO: Waterbrook, 2020), p 61.

Part 2

Merriam-Webster Dictionary.

Jennie Allen, *Restless: Because You Were Made for More* (Nashville, TN: W Publishing Group, an imprint of Thomas Nelson, 2013), p 146.

Jan Meyers, *The Allure of Hope: God's Pursuit of a Woman's Heart* (Colorado Springs, CO: NavPress, 2001) p 60.

Dictionary.com.

Bronnie Ware, *The Top Five Regrets of the Dying: A Life Transformed by the Dearly Departing* (*Australian Nurse Who Spent Several Years Working with Patients Who Had Less than Three Months to Live*). Internet article, www. bronnieware.com.

Julia Bekker, CTPost/Living, "The Difference between Settling vs. Compromising." April 2018.

Vocabulary.com.
Oxford Dictionary.

Beth Moore, *Sacred Secrets: Bible Study Experience* (Nashville, TN: Lifeway Press, 2014), p 93.

Macmillan Dictionary.

Karin Arndt, "A Hut of Her Own: The Fear of Being Alone," *Psychology Today,* April 2018.

Becky Van Valin, LSW, Eden Counseling.

"Going Beyond with Priscilla Shirer," 2019.

"80% of Thoughts Are Negative … 95% Are Repetitive." Faith Hope & Psychology, 2012.

Part 3

Statista: *32 Fascinating Beauty Industry Statistics.* dealsonhealth.net, May 2020.

Dying to Be Barbie: Eating Disorders in Pursuit of the Impossible. Rehabs.com.

How Women's "Perfect" Body Types Changed throughout History. thelist.com, March 2017.

A&E Television Networks, https://www.history.com/this-day-in-history/marilyn-monroe-is-found-dead

Lysa TerKeurst, *Uninvited: Living Loved When You Feel Less Than, Left Out, and Lonely* (Nashville, TN: Thomas Nelson, 2016), p 149.

Heart of Leadership: Lead Your World: *Statistics of Girls & Women's Self Esteem, Pressures & Leadership* (including Dove Self-Esteem Fund), www.heartofleadership.org.

Carey Lewis, Finding Beauty (What is Beauty & How Do You Get It?), www.**careylewis.us**, 2020

Stasi Eldridge quote, stasieldridge.com.

Sara Hagerty, *Unseen: The Gift of Being Hidden in a World That Loves to Be Noticed* (Grand Rapids, MI: Zondervan, 2017), p 210.

Part 4

Geology.com, *Where Do Diamonds Come From* (http://geology.com/articles/diamonds-from-coal); November 2014.

Diamondrocks.co.uk.
www.gia.edu.

Harriet Tubman, https://www.biography.com/activist/harriet-tubman.

Jay and Katherine Wolf, *Hope Heals: A True Story of Overwhelming Loss and Overcoming Love* (Grand Rapids, MI: Zondervan, 2016).

Christine Caine, *Unstoppable: Running the Race You Were Born to Win* (Grand Rapids, MI: Zondervan, 2014), pp 85–86, 95.

Lisa Bevere, *Lioness Arising: Wake Up and Change Your World* (Colorado Springs, CO: Waterbrook Press, 2010), p 187.

Jennie Allen, *Get Out of Your Head: Stopping the Spiral of Toxic Thoughts* (Colorado Springs, CO: Waterbrook, 2020), pp 56–57.

ABOUT THE AUTHOR

Sandra Coates is a speaker, fashion model, and mentor committed to sharing her faith while empowering women of all ages to walk confidently through life. The founder of a new movement, UNITED + TRU, Sandra has also worked for many years as a nurse manager for a pregnancy medical clinic. She has been actively involved in developing women's ministry at her church and mentored many leaders and girls through an international outreach ministry, Young Life. Sandra loves fashion, surfing, yoga, connecting with friends, new and old and making really good smoothies. She and her husband, Brett, an Executive Pastor, have three sons, a German shepherd named Anchor, and live in Virginia Beach.

Stay in Touch

Websites: sandracoates.com, unitedandtru.org
Instagram: sandracoates, unitedandtru
Facebook: Sandra Coates, unitedandtru
Youtube: UNITED and TRU

Printed in the United States
by Baker & Taylor Publisher Services